Brad Sugars, the founder of the business coaching profes ally known as the number 1 bu world. Born and bred in Brisbane, he graduated from Queensland University of Technology and now lives with his wife and kids in Las Vegas. With over 30 years of entrepreneurial experience, Brad has seen it all when it comes to starting, managing, and growing businesses. Now he's committed to translating his learnings and expertise into a message that helps other business owners, entrepreneurs, and marketers discover growth opportunities, avoid pitfalls, and stay ahead of the success curve. Brad has helped hundreds of thousands by speaking at events like BizX, joining numerous entrepreneurship podcasts and authoring 16 best-selling business books. This book was his idea, and he authored its original American version.

Kevin Whelan is the founder of Wealthbuilders. He is the leader of a thriving community of like-minded people who are committed to becoming financially independent. An entrepreneur himself, he saw that very few business owners ever sell their business and, as a result, don't get well rewarded for their blood, sweat and years. This included his own father who fell into the business owner's trap with very painful consequences. Spurred on by this, Kevin has created a step-by-step process for entrepreneurs to follow to create lasting wealth, so they do not have to rely solely on the income from their business. As an economist, author in his own right and having a wealth of experience in the UK, Kevin was asked to share some of his lessons and to ensure The Wealth Coach was made relevant for a UK audience.

IAN CHRISTELOW is the co-founder and chairman of ActionCOACH UK. The family business folding when he was young had a marked influence on Ian. When he came across Action's methodology and toolkit in 2001, he knew it would help prevent other companies from meeting the same fate. For this reason, Ian has dedicated the remainder of his life to helping other business owners avoid the same fate. Ian is of Yorkshire parentage, but of an Essex upbringing. Ian now lives with his family in rural Leicestershire and is a keen tennis player. His partner, Julie Wagstaff, started as an ActionCOACH franchise owner in Kettering back in 2005 and is now Managing Director for ActionCOACH UK.

SALLY ANNE BUTTERS owns Rev PR with her business partner Lucy Archer. ActionCOACH UK uses this multiple award-winning PR agency to promote its messages. As a client of ActionCOACH and an attendee of many of Brad Sugars' seminars, Sally developed a deep understanding of what this book wanted to convey and was a natural choice of editor; she also wrote some of the content and drove the project to completion.

The
WEALTH
coach

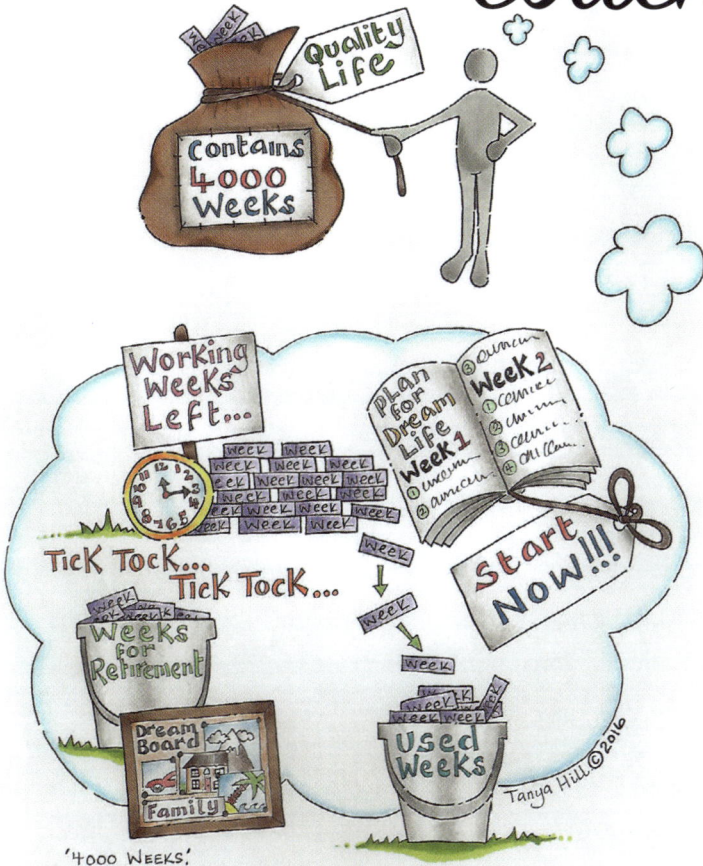

BRAD SUGARS • KEVIN WHELAN
IAN CHRISTELOW • SALLY ANNE BUTTERS

Publisher: CreateSpace Independent Publishing Platform

©2022 by Publisher

All rights reserved. Published 2022.

ISBN 978-1-915787-71-2

'4,000 Weeks' illustration by Tanya Hill: tanyahill@actioncoach.com

Printed in the UK by Biddles Books Limited, King's Lynn, Norfolk

From Ian Christelow:

This book is dedicated to my Dad, Alastair Donald Christelow, who had the courage not to die wondering, and set up his own business in pursuit of more choice for his family. He worked hard, played hard and left behind a wealth of happy memories, which live on.

Thank you for being my hero, friend and sounding board. You're in my thoughts every day and without your contribution this British story would never have happened…

Contents

Foreword

In British universities today, you can study everything from Acting to Zoology, yet three key elements in UK society remain barely touched upon in the UK education system:

1. The profession of selling;
2. How to practically build, run and sell a business; and
3. Wealth creation.

You can find thousands of helpful books to get you started on the first two subjects, but there's very little on wealth creation tailored to help people in the UK get their head around this subject of universal interest. So, we've adapted Bradley J. Sugars' story on wealth creation to suit British readers - let's face it, Oscar Wilde's and George Bernard Shaw's observations of differences between America and England from before the end of World War II, remain just as apt today! And we've made it shorter and punchier, as we're all too aware there are increasing demands on your time.

But if that's not enough to motivate you to complete this book, perhaps some inspiration from England's World Cup winning rugby coach will inspire you:

"I'd travel to the other side of the world to learn something which made me or my team better. Be a sponge not a rock. The day you stop learning is the day you risk being second best."

SIR CLIVE WOODWARD
paraphrased from his 2019 speech at BizX.

Coaching and educating people on how wealth happens is not an easy task, but then again, few worthwhile endeavours ever are. Transferring Brad Sugars' and Kevin Whelan's knowledge and expertise to others is a two-way street. Let's assume you wanted to make a complex dish for which only I had the recipe. Giving you the recipe would be simple. However, it would be up to you to shop for the ingredients, understand the directions (and, if needed, seek clarification) and be able to follow those directions. Most importantly, you would have to want to make the dish and get cooking! A little teaching from a world-class chef wouldn't go amiss either.

Fortunately, Brad & Kevin's recipe for wealth creation is simple and presented here in an easy-to-follow, entertaining story of two people who must start their wealth-building journey from scratch due to a financial wake-up call.

There are many roads to wealth but, as you'll find in the following chapters, some very tried and true principles work when you apply them patiently. These principles are your road map to wealth, whether you're starting your journey in your teens or sixties.

Creating wealth for yourself is not magic, and it's not down to luck. There is no get-rich-quick scheme, but it doesn't have to be a chore either. It is about learning, strategy, planning and persevering. Patience and self-discipline are key… *The Wealth Coach* is about to teach you how, and then it's up to you. Become wealthy or not. The choice is yours.

Introduction

It usually takes a catalyst for someone to take a structured path to wealth – true financial independence. This book takes you through a simple story to help put our steps to creating wealth into context. Your catalyst or Big Goal could be different from the characters in our story but your route to creating wealth will need these same steps of learning on how to not only create wealth but manage it too.

You'll follow a wealth creation journey for a brother and sister where the story begins with a sad but common situation happening to people throughout the UK right now. The story and characters are a work of fiction – any similarities to you or people you know are purely coincidental.

Lessons in this book will be highlighted on post-it notes. We recommend you stop and think at each one – how do they relate to you and your wealth creation journey? To help with understanding the journey, our lessons are split between the following:

Our wealth coach will explain these and their relevance throughout the book.

You have to manage your life. Just like in your career, you can delegate aspects of your life to others, but you must have overall knowledge and control. Your finances are one of the most important aspects you must manage to ensure a secure future.

Chapter 1

An end

Claire Spencer is 40 when her father, John, dies and her mother, Jenny, asks her to pay for his funeral. As everyone in the family expected, John had left everything to his wife in his will, but Jenny thought he would have a life insurance policy to pay for the funeral. John had been in the process of retiring at 65 when he found out he had cancer. The illness had progressed quickly and during that time, he'd hastily sold his three flower shops in and around Birmingham. The sales had paid off his debts but that was all. It was such a shock that Jenny and John had not had the time to talk about his funeral – Jenny had desperately hoped they wouldn't need to, and John was so angry at the world to be robbed of the retirement years he had been so looking forward to.

Just a couple of months before his diagnosis, John had signed the paperwork to take his private pension. He had taken 25% as a tax-free cash lump sum which he used to pay off the remainder of his mortgage and book the holiday of a lifetime he had always promised himself and Jenny. He was proud to be able to do that and ensure his wife would always have a roof over her head, no matter what the future held. But little did Jenny know that the annuity he chose to take on the other 75% of his pension would be cut to half the monthly payment should John pass away. Now Jenny would have to cope with this small monthly sum, even though his departure would not cut her bills down by the same proportion. The shock of her husband's departure was compounded by her realisation that he hadn't been legally obliged to discuss his pension choices with her. It was a sad state of affairs, but she was lucky to have a daughter who was successful in business who she could call on for help.

Claire had started a business four years ago, a floral sundries warehouse called Florist Extras. Her Dad's business was the inspiration for Florist Extras - she loved all the people she met through her Dad's business but was always concerned by the potential for waste with fresh flowers. Choosing a related business wholesaling everything but the fresh flowers was the perfect solution for her, and her Dad's flower shops were some of her first customers in those early days.

When her family got together, they didn't talk about money or business, they were usually celebrating a birthday or focusing on helping with one of their Dad's charity events. Everyone assumes Claire is quite well-off because of her fancy car and the restaurants she likes to eat at with her friends – her business must be doing very well. But Claire is shocked by the cost of quite a simple funeral and paying for it takes a huge chunk of her savings. She'd so far saved £25,000 towards a mortgage deposit and the £7,000 for the funeral really set back her plans for buying a house.

Let's be clear, John was not a bad chap, nor was he financially unaware but he just didn't get around to some of the essentials - it's a common situation so many people find themselves in. He also hadn't taken into consideration the worst-case scenario when taking decisions like that of his pension. With good intentions, he'd simply taken the pension offered by the company he'd been saving with for years.

Jenny's son, Mark, is three years younger than Claire and has a good job in IT. With two children and a wife working part time, Jenny doesn't consider him as an option to help pay for the funeral. She asks him instead to arrange the catering for the wake.

The funeral is attended by John's many friends including those from the charities he has supported over the years. Claire speaks to one of those, Frank, at the pub across from the church. Frank had met John at one of his fundraisers, as John was keen to support the hospice where his mother had passed away some years before.

Frank is the wealth coach in our story. He is 68 years old and started his career in a time when a job could be had for life and gave a fantastic final-salary pension, but he wasn't content to settle with that. In his early 20s, his employer sent him on a management course that blew his mind – it set him on a path where he was determined to help others in the same way.

Frank wasn't born into a wealthy family. His working-class family upbringing in Northumberland had taught him the values of education, hard work, and determination. Initially working through the ranks from his management position in an international management consultancy, spending time with clients on-site worldwide, he gained a huge level of knowledge to help businesses and developed a fantastic team of staff to support him. He was promoted to director level before branching out to start a management consultancy of his own. His business gained a great reputation and he soon expanded to a team of consultants - all trained personally by Frank. Frank found that delivering reports on improvements to be made was one thing, but many businesses struggled to implement the changes needed. He began testing an extension to his services where he coached business owners on a one-to-one basis, finding solutions to address the areas of concern his management consultants had raised. The work was really rewarding and, as his business expanded, he started to reinvest the profits by taking part or the whole of companies he knew he could grow substantially using his methods and selling them on once he'd greatly increased their value. During this time, he looked more into wealth creation and management, bringing those learnings into his coaching portfolio. His coaching evolved to showing business owners how to create wealth both inside and outside of their businesses. His own skills he'd developed in property investment and the connections he'd fostered, allowed Frank to fill his life with a balanced range of activities – some he did for money, some for interest, some for pleasure and some for a cause - and he loved seeing his clients go on to enjoy their lives too.

He'd spent the last 30 years splitting his time between speaking engagements, group coaching events and one-to-one coaching for business owners to help them get to grips with wealth creation. He'd developed a system for creating wealth which he had refined over the years to use in his coaching sessions. He didn't have to work now but he loved being a wealth coach, so it really wasn't like having a job at all. His own wealth had allowed him to spend more time on a passion of his - he'd started a charity called Folks who FUNdraise. He began with just one event a year to incorporate something really fun that would clear a minimum of £50,000 profit for a group of three charities close to his heart - a hospice near Newcastle, his local air ambulance and a veterans' association.

The Folks who FUNdraise had evolved to four events a year. Whilst the "Folks who" had been dropped from the name, the folks involved had multiplied with a board of trustees to manage the events and the charities who benefited from the £1million a year they raised had expanded too. John had been one of the team who brought the events to the Midlands. He gave his time generously but had never asked for any advice for his own business from Frank.

Whilst John had never become wealthy, he'd taken some of the steps that Frank would regularly advise his clients to take, but he just hadn't done them in the right order and lacked the knowledge to generate financial independence from his businesses. So, John was motivated to give back through his time, whereas Frank could give both his time and a proportion of his wealth too.

"Your Dad was a great friend and he'll be sorely missed," said Frank. "If there's anything I can do to help you and the family in the coming weeks, please let me know. I know today will be a blur for you, but you'll feel the effects of this for some time to come. Maybe we could do something through the charity to remember him?"

Chapter 2
A realisation

Whilst Claire is walking her dog, a cheeky Border Terrier called Baggins, the next day, she wonders how she can avoid ending up in the same position as her Dad when she reaches 65. In fact, she had hoped to retire much earlier than the traditional age. By the time she got to 65, with how things were going, the state pension age would be pushed back to 80! But whatever happened, she knew a state pension wasn't going to support the lifestyle she would like in retirement. She would never say this out loud to her family but, she certainly didn't want anyone else to have to pay for her funeral when she did die – she's feeling a bit gutted about having to start from scratch with her mortgage deposit again. Baggins didn't care, he's just looking out for squirrels to chase, lifting Claire's spirits.

It was her Dad who had taken her to his work in the holidays; she'd got to know the flower business and it had led her to start Florist Extras. She'd seen the long hours her Dad had put into his flower shops and, now she was in business herself, she'd wondered on several occasions whether it was all worth it. But she was generally a positive person and because she loved her company and the people it brought into her life, she decided to think about what she could do to boost her business and build up that house deposit in double-quick time.

Claire gets back to her business on Monday. Her floral sundries warehouse sells everything a flower shop or florist might need, except for the fresh flowers and plants. The warehouse is racked out and the shelves are full. The signage makes it easy for customers to browse and fill out order forms – she lets customers come in as they end up buying more when they can touch the silk flowers, the baskets and pottery or see the patterned ranges of cellophane wrapping. She's recently been working on displays at the end of each aisle to show how some of the products can be used together.

Her Warehouse Assistant, Rachel, comes around the corner from the office, with a mug of steaming coffee for Claire.

"How was your weekend, after the funeral on Friday?" asks Rachel. She's worked with Claire for the past two years. She has a daughter who she raises by herself and is thankful Claire allows her to work from 9am until 3pm every day, minimising the need for expensive childcare.

"I've been doing a lot of thinking Rach," replies Claire. "I've got some things to sort out this morning if you don't mind taking the mobile and covering the warehouse?"

Rachel takes the business mobile from Claire, gives Baggins a fuss, and gets on with her morning stock check.

Claire and Baggins head to the office and he settles down in bed in front of the heater. Claire sits down her coffee and decides to take a mental step back to look at her situation. She's a fan of lists, post-it notes and stationery in general. She begins with a list of observations about her finances.

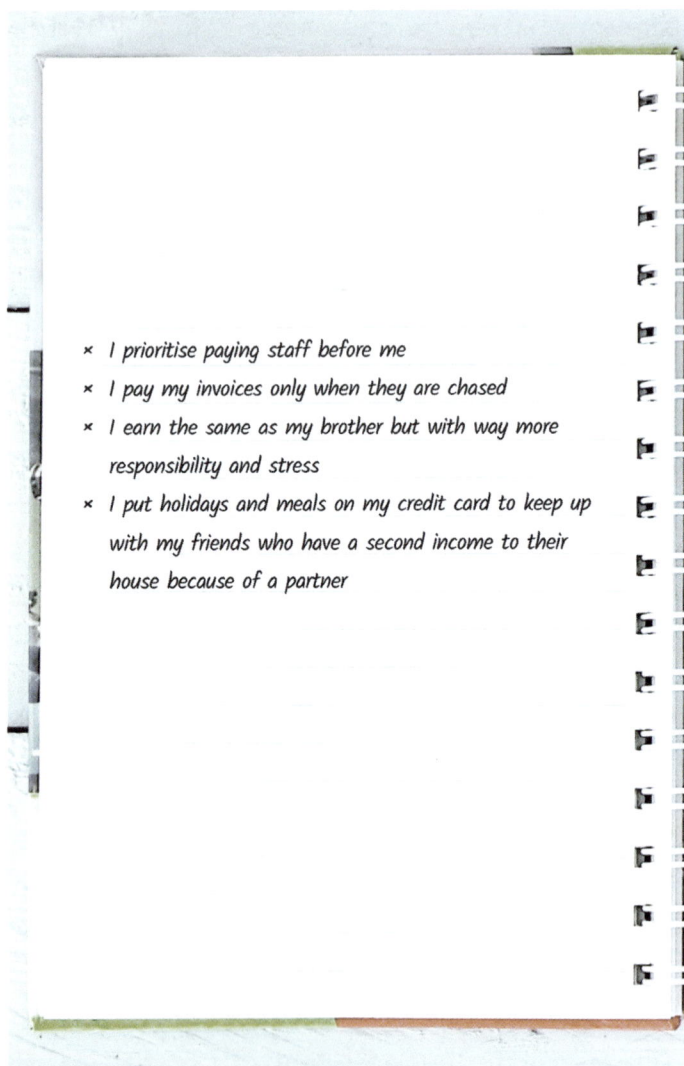

× I prioritise paying staff before me

× I pay my invoices only when they are chased

× I earn the same as my brother but with way more responsibility and stress

× I put holidays and meals on my credit card to keep up with my friends who have a second income to their house because of a partner

Her mind wanders on the last point. She's had so little free time, she'd not bothered to even think about dating for nearly a year – she will never have her own family at this rate. She gets back to her lists, the next one is the roles she fulfils in the business, wondering if she could bring Rachel in to help her more.

- × **HR** – *recruitment, retention and reviewing*
- × **Finance** – *banking, payroll, bookkeeping and liaising with the accountant*
- × **Marketing & sales** – *networking, advertising*
- × **Buyer** – *choosing the right products for the warehouse*
- × **Logistics** – *overseeing deliveries and sometimes stepping in for local deliveries*
- × **Managing Director** – *I should be spending more time on this!*

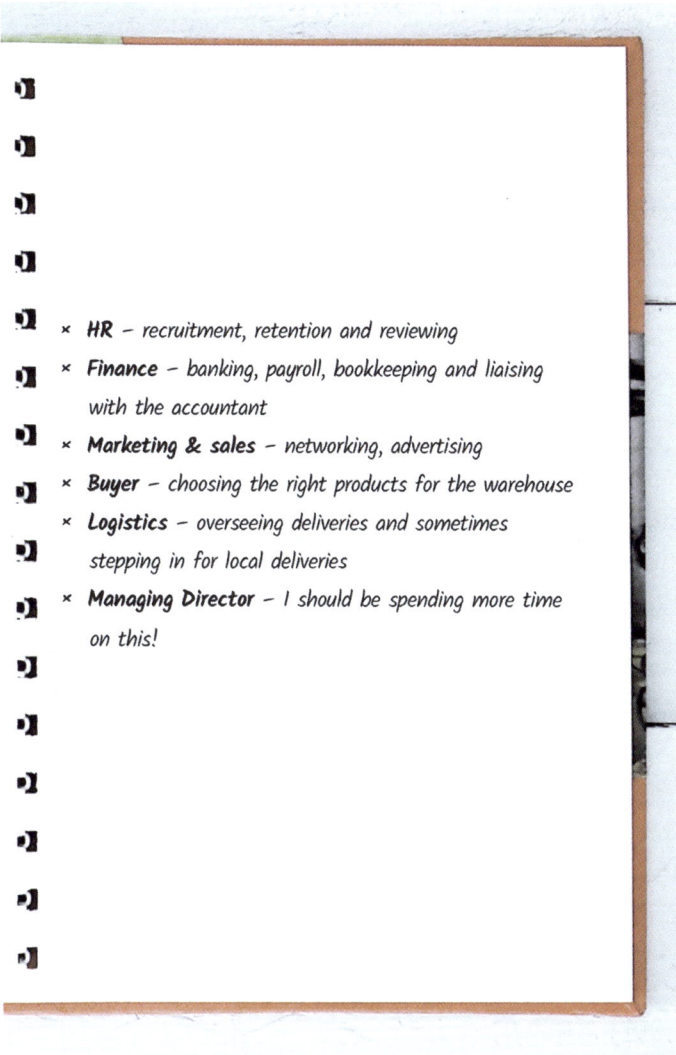

Reading back through the list, Claire is sure she has missed things out but yet again, she's struck by the thought that her brother has just one role and still gets paid the same as her. She has to do something now, she feels like she is already running out of time. As the panic sets in, she remembers Frank's kind offer when they spoke at the wake.

Did he really mean it? There was only one way to find out, she calls her Mum and asks for Frank's number from her Dad's address book and dials the number.

Frank is surprised to hear from Claire so soon but is more surprised to hear that her call is not about the charity. Claire rounds up the situation she has found herself in. Frank empathises with Claire - he knows the challenges that business owners face with the large majority never realising the true potential from their business.

"I'd like to know what I can do to put myself in a stronger position financially. I want to make sure I don't end up with another 25 years of this, only to find I can't afford to retire. Is there some way I can do it and keep a semblance of work-life balance?" asks Claire.

"If you're really serious about creating wealth, then I can help you. I have a full day today so I can't talk right now but let's set up a meeting. There's something I need you to do before we meet," says Frank. Claire grabs a new notebook which is covered in an old-fashioned map of the world. She writes the first thing that will begin their work together.

I need a great big reason! The only way I will achieve anything major is when I have a great big reason. A WHY? Burning in my head or my heart. OR both.

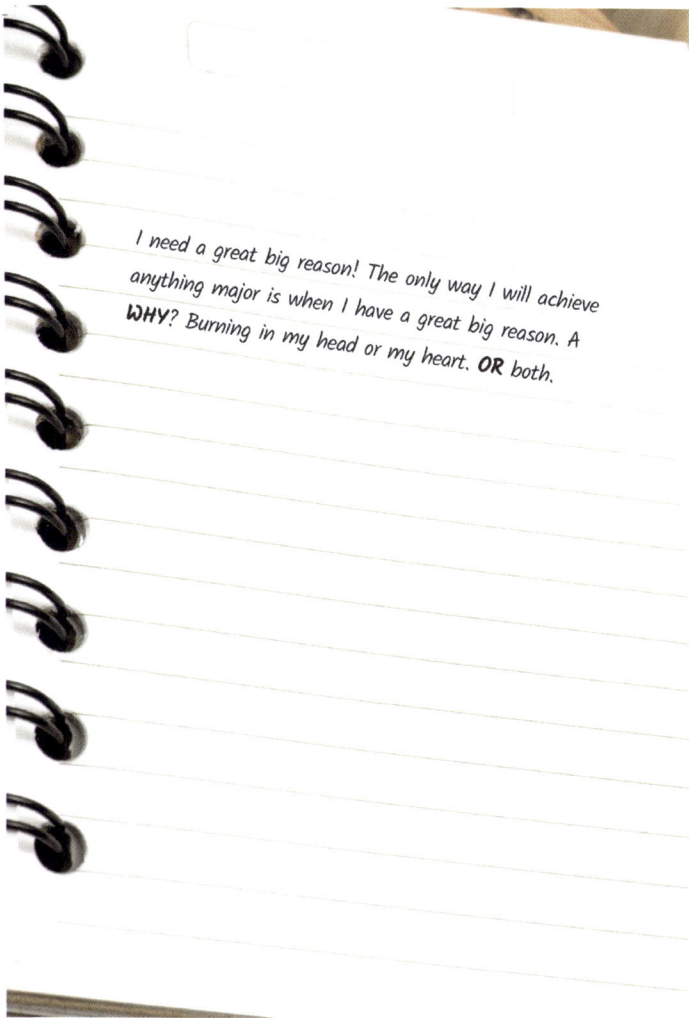

"Sometimes it's difficult to get started on your Why, so try focusing on these questions to gain some clarity. What gets you jumping out of bed in the morning? What worries you so it keeps you from sleeping soundly at night? What would friends say about you at your 70th birthday party? How do you want to be remembered?"

Frank finishes the call, "Don't confuse the process of how to get wealthy with the reasons or motivations of why to get wealthy. Right now, focus on the why, not the how."

Claire puts her new pad to one side and spends the rest of the day thinking about all the reasons why she would want to be wealthy. There are so many! Is her big reason going to make her sound materialistic? She likes nice things but she's no princess! If she looks back at Frank's achievements, they seem to come from a more altruistic place but maybe that is because she did not know him when he was first becoming wealthy.

Rather than wait until the meeting and waste Frank's time, Claire emails him to ask if she is on the right track with her Why. She has seen wealthy people get even richer, but she is concerned about how her Why will help her get there when she doesn't even have any savings left. And is her Why big enough?

> Hi Frank,
>
> Looking forward to our meeting but I'm worried my Why is too limited? I doubt it's anything like yours or Bill Gates', if he has a Why!
>
> At the moment, mine is: I don't want someone else to have to pay for my funeral. I want to be able to foster a child as a single person. That means I have to have a home big enough to accommodate at least one child and be able to be at home during school holidays without worrying about my business or bank account running low.
>
> I understand that my Why could change if my relationship status changes but want to foster and feel I should construct my Why

for my current situation. I'm sorry if these questions seem basic or stupid!

Best wishes

Claire

Frank's meeting with Claire is still a few days away. He often finds his clients struggle with their Why – some do not know where to start and others go as far as wanting world peace. Rather than leave Claire to worry, he sends her the first page of his coaching notes on how people choose reasons Why. Claire has left her notepad at work and so she grabs a set of red post-it notes from the kitchen and write down the key points from Frank's notes.

I can have either positive or negative reasons. My **WHY** – or big reason – can be focused on a positive goal I really want, or it can be about getting away from a negative situation that causes me pain.

LEVEL 1 GOALS:

My negative reasons WHY are short-term motivators. Most people start with a negative reason – to prove something to someone, to get out of debt or to quit a bad job or relationship. Basically, I may want to get out of some sort of pain, but that will generally only motivate me short term.

There is a formula for change - a formula for making big changes happen in your business and your life:

$$(D \times V) + FS) \times S > R$$

To Claire's relief, Frank's notes explain this formula for change in detail, breaking it into its separate elements to she can start to understand its power.

Dissatisfaction (D)

You need to feel at least some unhappiness with the current situation to make a change - the more pain you feel, the more likely you will change something. Your Why is the key to creating an urgency to make the changes. If it is 10/10 important to you, it will feel like taking action to change the current situation feels like a do-or-die importance.

Vision (V)

The human brain is wired to move away from pain and towards pleasure. The vision part of the formula is pleasure focused. The more excited you are about the vision of what business or life would be like after you have made the changes, the more likely you are to do whatever it takes to make the changes. And if your vision is filled with enough passion, it will ignite sparks in the people around you. Again, your Why plays a big part in driving your feeling higher.

First Steps (FS)

This is how clear you are on what steps you need to take to make your desired change happen. Working with a world-class wealth coach and a world-class business coach can really help you to develop a step-by-step plan to create the business and life you dream of.

Support (S)

Every New Year's Eve millions of people resolve to get fit; hundreds of thousands are serious enough to join a gym to help them achieve their level 1 goal; and tens of thousands hire a personal trainer who works out where they are currently, finds out where they want to get to and by when and creates a plan for them to achieve that, as well as teaching them how to do the exercises correctly and providing external motivation. Most people will let themselves down but are much less inclined to let down someone else. Occasionally, you'll meet someone so strong-minded and self-disciplined that support is much less of a factor for them in this formula compared to the rest of us humans. So, if you want to stack the odds heavily in favour of achieving your goal, you need supportive people around you who are clued up as to what you need to do to succeed.

Resistance to Change (R)

This is everything that might stand in your way of making a change i.e. lack of time, financial resource, negative people who de-energise you.

It is useful to score each element to see how likely change is and also start to think about what you could do to increase each part of the formula to the left of the greater than sign. Discussing this with a mentor can help come up with the easiest ways but I have put in some hypothetical numbers to illustrate how useful the formula is:

$$((D \times V) + FS) \times S > R$$
$$((10 \times 8) + 9) \times 30\% > 50\%$$

Using the example of someone who resolves to get fit, is 10/10 fed up with their lack of fitness, 8/10 excited about a fit version of themselves, 9/10 clear on what they need to do to achieve that, 30% strength of support around them and facing 50% resistance to making the changes, then the formula indicates the chances are they won't get there:

10 x 8 = 80 + 9 = 89 x 30% = 26.7 which is lower than 50.

As their mentor, I would be getting them to focus on the two areas with the most potential to swing the equation in favour of achieving their fitness goal which in this example would be increasing their support and lowering their resistance to change. It could be hiring a personal trainer increases their support to 90% and paying someone to do their ironing frees up their time enough to lower their resistance to change to 25%:

10 x 8 = 80 + 9 = 89 x 90% = 80.1 which is way higher than 25 and therefore means success becomes almost inevitable.

Perturbation:
For growth to happen, I need to be under pressure. Sometimes this pressure is negative. However, with goal-setting or working with a mentor, I can make it positive.

LEVEL 2 GOALS:

My positive reasons WHY are longer-term motivators. Generally, most people never make the transition to positive WHYs. Once they are out of pain, they stop. Average is okay for them. I need to find a reason to move from average to the best I can be, so I keep progressing long-term with positive reasons.

LEVEL 3 GOALS:

Legacy goals are about leaving a mark long after I've gone. The kind of goal which inspires others and makes a difference I can be proud of.

Frank's notes continue.

Do you have a bucket list of dreams and goals? Those deeper-meaning goals around relationships, giving back, health, parenting, legacy and financial independence are great drivers. This is the first step to building true wealth and making your dreams your reality. You might not know how to achieve these goals when you first set out. You might even feel that you don't currently possess the skills to be capable of achieving them but that's the whole point - you've got to grow into these goals.

Leaders in all arenas use positive reasons. As a business owner, a great vision for your business can motivate you, inspire great people to join you and inspire your team to do more than they need to do to keep their job.

The only stupid questions are the ones you don't ask.

Claire writes the last lesson
on another red post-it and
decides she will stick these
into her notepad first thing
tomorrow.

I've only got one shot – one life.
That is approximately 4,000 weeks
(77 years) to do the best I can.
Why would I want to waste it
being less than I can be? I need
to make the most of the gift of
life and be the best **ME** I can
be. Some people didn't get that
gift today.

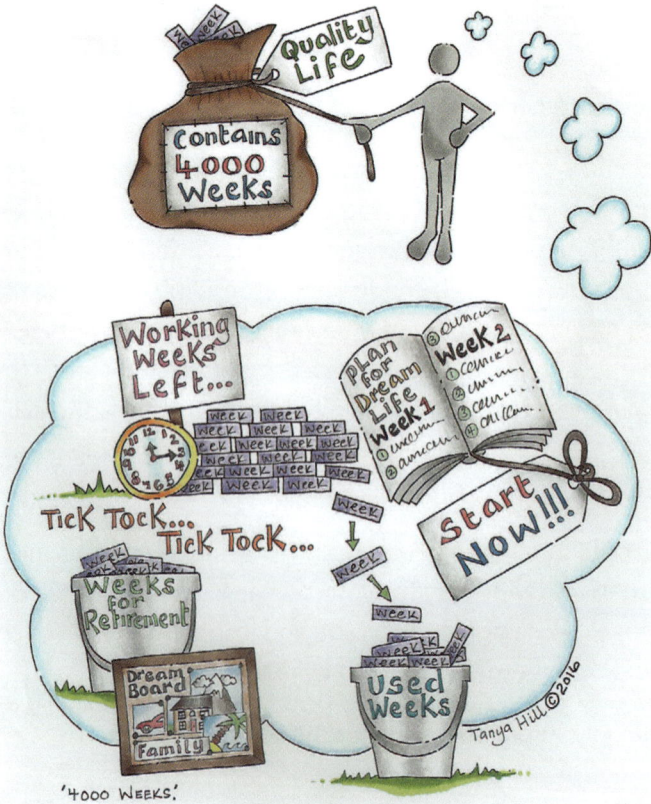

'4000 Weeks.'

Claire thinks back to her Dad. Did he make the most of his life? She will always remember the good times but, honestly, she knows he could have done more. This isn't about money but learning to understand, create and manage wealth will set her up to do more in life for others, as well as herself. She just needs to form a picture of what that would look like.

Chapter 3

A new start

Claire's first meeting with Frank comes around quickly. Frank is on one of his seminar tours and has booked them a meeting room in a hotel near New Street Station in Birmingham. After settling down with both a coffee and water, Frank sees Claire has come prepared to take notes. She has brought a notepad, several pens and post-it notes, as well as her laptop. Claire explains that she's decided to add the coloured post-it notes in for lessons and write her own observations in between and shows Frank what she's done so far.

"I'm going to outline the coaching process with you today and see if you're someone I could coach going forwards. I don't coach everyone who asks me and by the end of this session, I'll have a good idea if you're committed enough to the process to join me on my wealth programme. People normally pay several thousand pounds to follow this programme but, if I think you're a good fit, I'm going to coach you for free because of all the great years of friendship I had with your Dad.

"Building wealth is a step-by-step process – you have to be committed to the process - for some it can take 10 years to reach their goal and others have done it in five years. My coaching is very different from the teachers you remember in school or a mentor you've had in the past. The only failure with me is the failure to participate fully. If you're up for the challenge, you can learn some life lessons which will propel you to a great future - a future you design according to your dreams and goals. You must give this 100% or we're just wasting our time. The question is, are you in?"

Claire pauses for a moment's reflection and replies, "100% yes. It's reassuring this is going to take five to 10 years. Everything you've taught me so far makes sense and I want to learn more."

Frank nods in approval and gets started straight away.

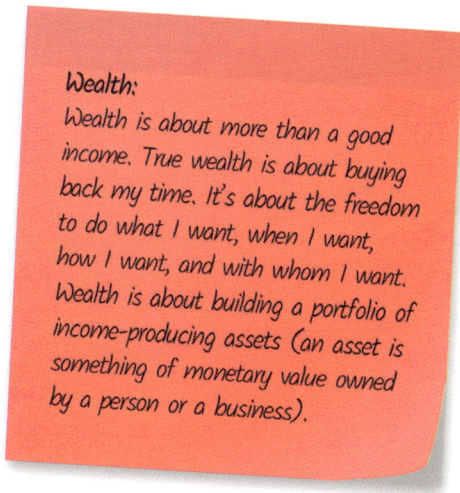

> **Wealth:**
> Wealth is about more than a good income. True wealth is about buying back my time. It's about the freedom to do what I want, when I want, how I want, and with whom I want. Wealth is about building a portfolio of income-producing assets (an asset is something of monetary value owned by a person or a business).

"It looks to me like your big reason is to become free. Coming up with your Why can take some time. To finalise your big reason, you want to consider it from a slightly different angle. Wealth isn't just about having lots of money."

Wealth is about freedoms.
- *Time* – free to spend my time as I choose
- *Finance* – free to use money for more than standard expenses
- *Relationships* – free to be with the people I like or love
- *Creativity* – free to take my ideas forward
- *Purpose* – free to achieve my goals
- *Location* – free to live life in any place I choose.

"Wealth creates freedoms that bring a level of joy and contentment to your life which impacts wellbeing and health too. You now have to decide what is your reason to choose wealth and what freedoms you choose to develop."

Chapter 4

Choosing freedom

On the train home, Claire starts listening to Frank's podcasts from episode one - a great use of her journey time. She chooses three freedoms – finance, relationships and time. She has her second meeting with Frank tomorrow before he flies up to Edinburgh to continue his tour. She updates her Why to:

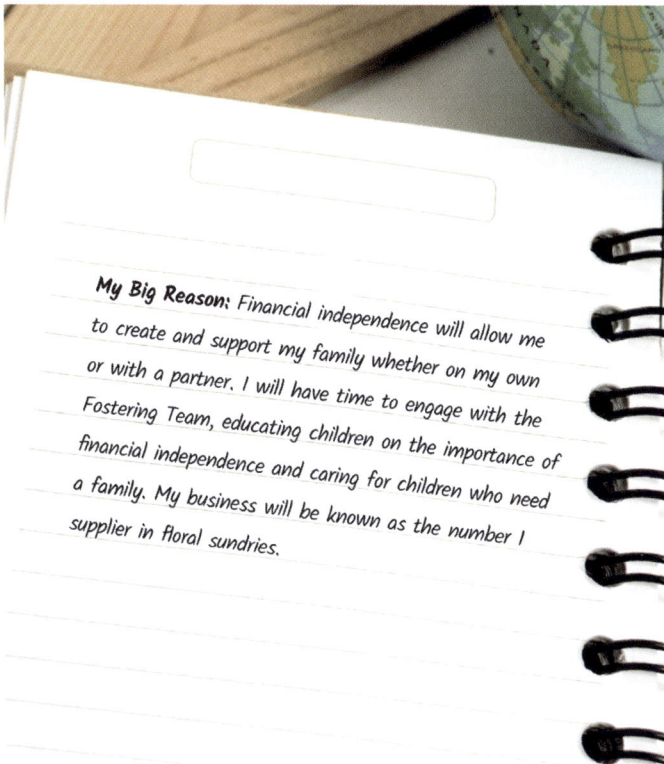

My Big Reason: Financial independence will allow me to create and support my family whether on my own or with a partner. I will have time to engage with the Fostering Team, educating children on the importance of financial independence and caring for children who need a family. My business will be known as the number 1 supplier in floral sundries.

It is day two of her coaching session with Frank and Claire. She's pleased with her new Why - she thinks it includes more positive and legacy goals compared to her first attempt which was definitely more negative goals. But Frank has noticed one thing that has slipped into her Why which isn't supposed to be there.

"Being known as the number one supplier in your industry would be something you may wish to include in your business' vision statement but it's not something to focus on during your wealth journey."

> Wealth isn't about being in competition with others. The freedoms I choose and the income I want are unique to me - I should not be comparing myself to anybody else. Concentrate on achieving my own objectives and don't look over my shoulder at others.

That now sounds obvious to Claire, but she still has a worry at the back of her mind. She's wondering how she'll keep up with everything her friends do - the holidays, cars, good food - and achieve this big Why. She doesn't have the time for all of the expensive trips and luxury holidays her friends take, but she does like one decent holiday a year and what will her friends think if she cuts back any more on her time with them?

She asks Frank, "How can I save money without impacting on my lifestyle?"

"Let's talk about saving first. This is a very common question I get Claire and I want to stress from the very beginning, you cannot save your way to wealth. You must expand your means and I will show you how to do this over the course of the coming months," Frank continues.

"Now, going back to what you said about your lifestyle, do you talk about money with your friends? I'm not normally a betting man but I'd bet £100 on your perception of your friends' wealth is wrong. People buy things they can't afford, paying one credit card off with another. Once you've paid for your monthly essentials from your income, if you don't have the money left to pay for these extras, you shouldn't be buying them.

"Imagine if your Dad hadn't managed to pay off his overdraft just before he died. Now imagine if your Dad had passed away 20 years earlier. If he couldn't pay off his debts with one month's income, his family would have been left with them to deal with too - managing their grief plus funeral costs, credit cards and overdraft, children at university and a wife trying to pick up the reins of a business she's previously had little to do with."

Claire agrees and suddenly starts thinking about her brother who probably falls into the category that Frank has just described. She tries to focus back on herself and her limited time with Frank.

Frank is happy Claire has shown commitment to the process. He's using these two meetings to bring in the first foundation for building wealth - mindset. He's sure Claire is suitable to join his programme but has more to share before they finish today.

"Remember, wealth is important, but never something to lose respect over. Make sure all your decisions and actions are ones you'll be proud of. I think you'll want to take some more notes."

My actions earn me my reputation. I want my epitaph to read, "I gave everything my absolute best." When my life is over, imagine how proud people will feel about me. This is the sort of life I want to have.

My only job in life is to be the best ME I can be. I've been given a certain set of talents and skills, and I have no right but to use them to be the best I can be, because that's how I am designed.

We have no choice but to choose: wealth, middle class, or poverty.

"It can take the same amount of effort to choose right or wrong, good or bad, wealthy or poor, best or average. So, why not choose what's in your best interest?

"The next step is to think about the number that would set you free."

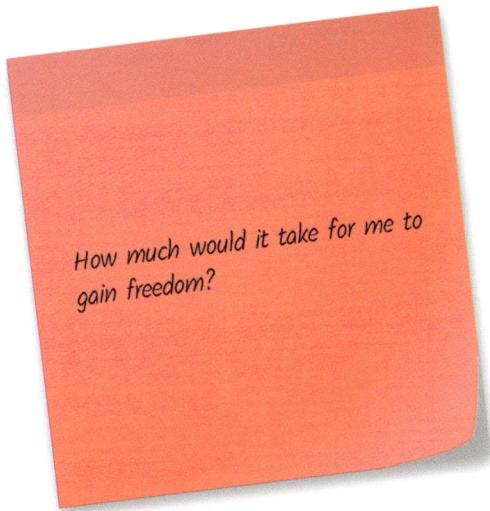

How much would it take for me to gain freedom?

"If you stopped working tomorrow, how long would it take for things to unravel? What would sustain you financially? Wealth can only be measured by income that recurs, not when you trade money for your time. Trading time for money is temporary, recurring income can be permanent but needs management - remember, there is no such thing as a passive income. We need to measure your wealth now and your progress towards milestones on the way to the level of wealth you want."

Aim for:

1st Financial security
2nd Financial independence

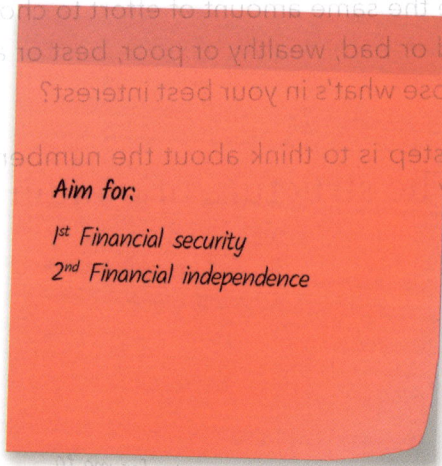

"Setting milestones will make it easier to reach each station on the way and stay motivated, as opposed to purely aiming for your destination of immense wealth and not celebrating or feeling good about yourself until you're there. We've gone through a lot this morning. Let's meet up at the same time next week."

Claire has made a good start in her notebook and packs away. Now Frank has said they will meet next week, she realises she's been accepted as part of his wealth coaching programme. She knows there's a lot more to learn, but she feels relieved to have someone like Frank to guide her on this journey.

Chapter 5
The structure of building wealth

It's never too late to take the advice of a wealth coach. Claire is coming up to her 41st birthday and she's excited to take the journey to wealth. She feels invigorated at work but doesn't exactly know how she can make this passion a practical force for results. It's the first thing Claire asks Frank about at their next session, reaching for her notebook, pens and post-it notes as Frank begins to explain.

> There are no get-rich-quick schemes. This is why people who win the lottery are usually broke in just a year or two. The dictionary is the only place where 'earn' comes before 'learn'. In the real world, if your level of learning is less than your level of wealth, you need to learn fast or your wealth will soon drop to your level of learning.

"Millions of people in the UK play the lottery, where almost all will lose their stake in the hope of winning millions. They repeat this week after week, just living their life in hope. This is not a wealth plan. If you really want to play a lottery, how about playing one where you're guaranteed to get your stake back even if you don't win a big prize? You can invest in Premium Bonds from as little as 25 pounds and have the chance to win a tax-free cash prize of up to one-million pounds, plus you can get your stake back with just a month's notice.

"If you don't have the knowledge to manage a large sum of money, it's easily spent and can leave very little lasting impact. You have to learn before you earn."

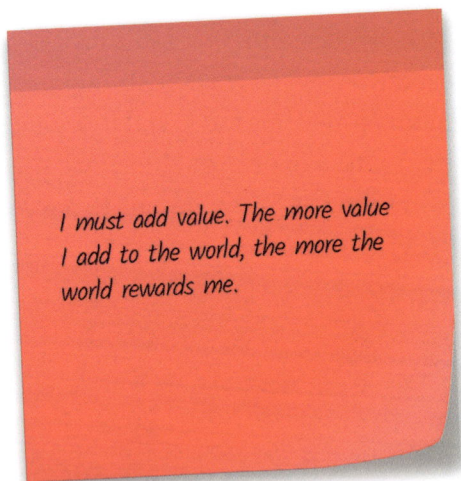

I must add value. The more value I add to the world, the more the world rewards me.

"Typically, there are three groups of people when it comes to being wealthy: those who never truly believe it will happen to them; those who think it might be nice and hope it will happen one day; and those who are committed to doing whatever it takes to make wealth happen for them. Three types of people who have no hope, hope or commitment.

"I really like the way you are showing commitment, Claire. Writing things down, not just typing or trying to remember, greatly reinforces learning. I'm about to explain the structure of building wealth to you and I think you'll find a great use for your different colours of post-it notes. There is no use doing something until you know what to do and why you're doing it.

"So, imagine your dream house. First of all, you wouldn't try to build it yourself, would you? Can you do the architect drawings, dig the foundations, and install the plumbing and electrics?"

Claire jokes, "I wouldn't even paint the walls – I'd get more paint on myself!"

"That's just why I recommend using experts for completing tasks where you're not the best person to do them. And just like building your dream house, there's a step-by-step process, from the ground to the chimney, for building wealth – regularly employing the help of experts along the way.

"Whenever you're trying to build wealth, it's important to recognise wealth is a flow - it represents a flow of value and the word's origins are in the Latin word 'currens', which means running or flowing. Grasp both your fists as if you're clutching all the money you have as tightly as you can. Now consider how hard it is to receive money when you're in this position. You're always having to create value through parting with your money and/or time and then money flows to that value. But before focusing on the flow of value, you need to understand your own personal flow.

"I'll send you a link to an online profiling tool which will help you to understand where your natural strengths as a business owner lie - your entrepreneur profile. Some people are more inclined to think creatively, whereas others are all about the details. It's important to recognise your entrepreneurial personality type so you can focus on the activities which get you into your flow each day. Understanding your personal flow then gives you the clarity on who you need in your team to take care of the tasks which you aren't so good at and clarity on the areas you are going to need to double down your focus and efforts on to get right while you find the right person to look after those areas.

"Once you've got the results from the profiling tool, we'll talk more about your personal flow. Now we're going to move onto the four simple principles of wealth building."

Claire takes note of the four principles Frank shares with her.

There are 4 simple principles.

1) **Foundation:** Mindset

2) **Foundation:** Finance

3) **Structure:** Assets

4) **Roof:** Protect your assets with a watertight cover

"Think about the first foundation as digging deep to develop a wealth mindset. Then at ground level, we have the finance foundation where we learn the basics that will serve you well throughout your journey to wealth. We'll then move on to above ground where we build a structure of assets. You may choose different assets to create wealth so everyone's journey may look slightly different, but the structure is always the same. Then you need a roof to ensure your structure stays watertight with a cover including a will and insurances.

"Have you considered that there's no ceiling to the amount of wealth that can be created? Whether it's a little or a lot, we all need a roof. A roof is a fundamental structure to any building. One of the first things a good architect or a good builder will want anyone to do is make a structure watertight because that keeps it safe. So, the protection of your assets and the legal organisation of your business is essential.

"Now this is going to be fresh in your mind after losing your Dad, but whenever we have assets, we want to make it clear how these pass on to others when we pass on ourselves. The key is not to wait to create your roof. As your wealth increases, you'll want to add to your roof and strengthen it as circumstances in life change. You've had direct experience of someone not getting around to making a will and organising life insurance. Whether you're a business owner or employee, lots of people just don't get around to doing that and in most cases it's such a simple thing to make a will. A will is a way of saying, if something happens to me, I would like this to be the flow of the assets I own when I'm no longer here.

"Now, it's equally important to think about how you manage the flow of your assets when you're alive but not able to make decisions for yourself, most commonly due to illness. There's a combination of ways you can do this. One is called power of attorney. In law there are two types of power of attorney - one over financial assets and one for medical decisions. So, if you were to become sick or disabled and unable to make decisions, these documents would come into play and clarify your wishes.

"Imagine an example where a couple worked in a business together, one person leading the business whilst the other was helping part time with admin and support. If the person driving the business got seriously ill, it's been known for a bank to be uncooperative because there's nobody to sign documents. So, the power of attorney is a living document saying, if something happens to me and I can no longer take care of myself in terms of making decisions, somebody else can do so. Simple documents which cost only a few hundred pounds to draw up but can eliminate some of the hurdles when life throws you a curve ball.

"I know I'm not talking about the most pleasant or cheery scenarios here but, nonetheless, they're important to raise with you. I know you don't have a business partner at the moment or children but if you get these fundamentals in place to create a watertight roof now, it'll be easier to amend them when your life changes than start from scratch then, and, in the meantime, you'll have cover for how your circumstances are now.

"There's another part of the roof which can put a spanner in the works and that's informal business agreements - the

The structure of building wealth

shake of a hand replacing good business practise. It may feel like the British thing to do, taking someone at their word, but I recommend getting professional contracts drawn up including a shareholder agreement if you decide to bring in business partners. It can seem a lot to keep up with the admin on these, especially if they cover differing periods with renewal dates so keep a log of them and review them regularly as part of your financial MOT.

"The final key aspect of the roof is insurance. Most people who think about taking care of their loved ones when they die, also tend to take out something to protect themselves in the event of their death - normally a life insurance policy. I'm not saying you should or shouldn't have one, but there's certainly a place for insurance if you've got a big mortgage or if you want to make sure people are taken care of if you're the breadwinner.

"One last thing on preventing a leaky roof relates to life insurance policies. Most people pay for those policies out of taxed income. They earn the money, pay the tax, and they pay the premium personally. But what if you could have the government pay towards the premium and reduce the net costs? Do you think that might be interesting?"

Claire nods her head, "That would be pretty smart."

"Yes exactly, smart people do that. It's called Relevant Life Cover - not that other life cover is irrelevant, it's just the terminology we use in the wealth coaching profession. It's a type of insurance you take out as a business owner.

"All these aren't complicated but, in the drift of life, people get busy, become complacent and don't get around to putting the essential roof structure in place. Let's not fall into this trap, let's get this done. When everything is watertight, you'll have peace of mind so you can focus on building your assets.

"We've been looking at the mindset foundation so far. Why don't you keep your red post-it notes for our lessons on mindset and use a different colour for the lessons in each of the other 3 principles?"

"Great," says Claire. "I'll use them like this."

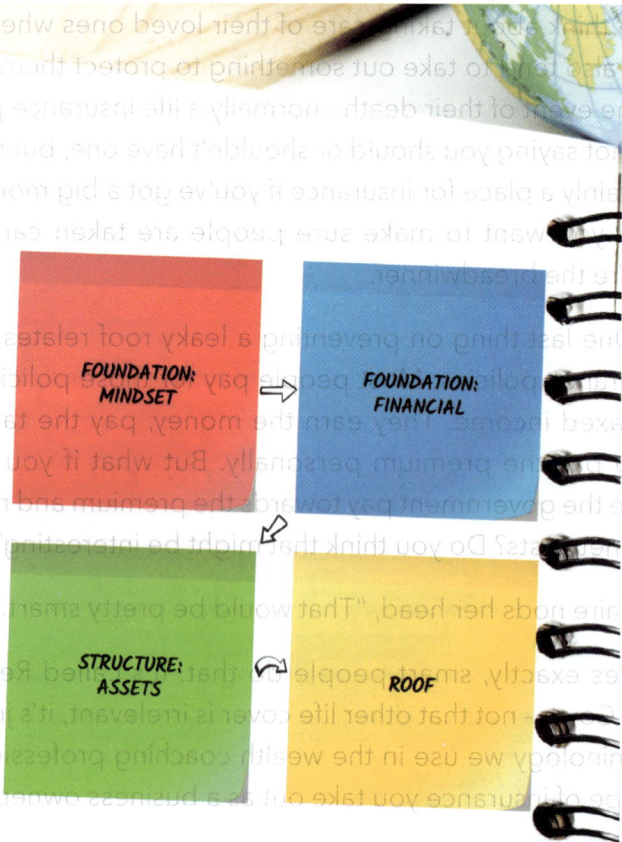

"Nice idea, Claire. So, let's move on to the second foundation - finance. Let me start with cashflow and capital."

Cashflow:
Most careers start with an active income from going to work 9 to 5 Monday to Friday – my goal is to turn my active income into a large passive income for myself over time.

"If you climb the cashflow ladder, you'll be better off than most, even if you do nothing more and never progress beyond a large cashflow."

Cashflow ladder:
As my experience and knowledge grow, I can move up the ladder and watch both my active and passive incomes grow.

Capital:
I started with no capital and my aim is to build it up over time, so I have a solid asset backing.

> *I must consider my Personal Flow – recognise what I'm good at and where viable, bring in other people to fill in the gaps. Just like when building a dream house.*

"Remember I sent you the entrepreneur profiling tool to work out your strengths and weaknesses when it comes to building wealth? We call this being in flow. You'd recognise times when you've been in your flow because time seemed to fly, and you'll remember people commenting on how you're a natural at whatever you were doing at the time. From the online profiling tool, you came out with a wealth profile of Creative & Connected. Your wealth strategy should therefore focus on connecting with people.

"I'm going to share with you lessons as and when you need to learn them. We're still learning the foundations of finance here so make sure these lessons are on your blue post-it notes Claire, not green. For now, there are four main assets I want to talk about, along with their foundation and roof. These income-producing assets are the walls of our dream house."

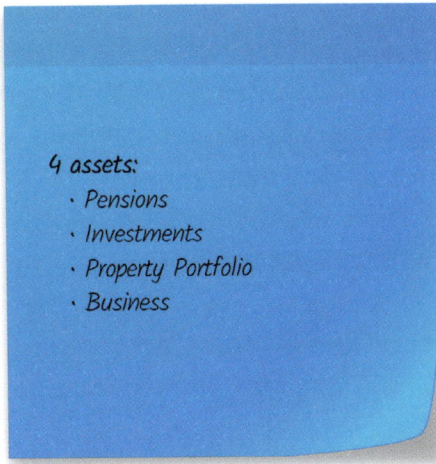

4 assets:
- Pensions
- Investments
- Property Portfolio
- Business

Frank draws a simple picture of a house on a blank sheet of paper.

"Most people, like your Dad, will have a house, a pension and an investment, something like an Individual Savings Account (ISA) or a few shares. Business and property portfolio assets are sometimes referred to as pillars because a person can elevate the value of that asset. Building a property portfolio is probably the one that you'll know quite a lot about from when you first played Monopoly as a kid and through all the shows on TV these days. You're not just living in a home, you're owning properties whether they're commercial or residential, for other people to pay rent.

"Owning a business is an asset when it creates ongoing profits or royalties or some form of ongoing income, but what you really want to achieve is a business that does all that even if you're not working in it day-to-day. A real business is a commercial, profitable enterprise that works without you. You could also include intellectual property with your business asset - that's when you create and capitalise on an income stream from what you know, often known as royalties. So, learning materials, training and systems can be packaged and repurposed to generate an ongoing revenue, without you having to be there; a franchise is an example of you packaging all of that and a proven business model into several streams of income i.e. franchise licence fees and royalties. At the heart of wealth building is the principle of collaboration - that means the generation of wealth by combining your skills, time and effort with other people's. They bring something to the table, so do you and you'll share in the value of that asset.

"Interestingly, in the same way you can grasp some of the fundamentals of property investing through playing

Monopoly, you can learn most of the basics of business through a boardgame called 'Leverage' – growing up, my kids actually preferred it to Monopoly, and it can be just as enjoyable and educational for business owners."

Claire jots down an action point to play Leverage and quickly notes she has two assets – her small pension and her business. She can't secure a mortgage yet because she doesn't have a deposit. Her brother also has two assets - a pension and an investment in an ISA. With her mind on her brother, she says goodbye to Frank. She wants to share what she's learned about the usual mistakes people make and much more with Mark, so she invites herself round for dinner.

Chapter 6
It's never too late to choose wealth

It's one month since the funeral. Claire has brought Baggins with her, so her nephews take him out for a walk after dinner while she sits with Mark and his wife, Sophie. Claire explains how she's come to a decision on her future and wonders if Mark has any plans.

"Well, Soph and I are paying our mortgage easily, we get a couple of holidays a year with the kids and, as long as they're well behaved, they don't miss out on the latest toys," he responds.

"But what about when you retire? What have you got planned to make sure, heaven forbid, Sophie isn't left in the same boat as Mum?" asks Claire.

"I've got a workplace pension and we got life insurance after what happened with Dad. I'm not sure there's much else I could do, sis?"

Claire explains about the two assets - pensions and investments - most people have, what Mark's options might be to create more wealth, so they do not simply 'get by' later in life. Then talk moves on to whether Mark can make it to the next FUNdraise event.

"I don't think I can make it, sis. By the time I'm back from work on Friday evening, I'll have missed the first hour. You'll have to represent the family on this one."

Claire says goodbye to her brother and his family, grateful for the company her dog provides when she is back at home - it's quiet compared to the busy home she's spent the evening in.

It doesn't take long for Mark to choose wealth too. Claire is back at work – it is Friday afternoon. Mark has had another week of train delays and cancellations with more time to think about what they spoke about. He texts her to say he needs to talk.

Mark's job is in IT, working for a large telecoms provider. He's well paid, but he must keep up with the fast developments in tech and feels like there are younger staff who might jump over him on the way up the promotional ladder.

They meet for coffee on a Sunday morning – the only day Claire gets off work. He explains how he ran the figures and his pension does not fill him with enthusiasm - certainly not enough to support him and his wife if they wanted to afford a decent retirement. There would be nothing left over if they wanted to treat their future grandkids and he's not going to be able to save up now he can see their boys are likely to need some help through university. They might only be 10 and 13 now but time will fly by. What can he do to become wealthy when he's nearly 38 and has a job that pays the bills but not much else?

"Don't worry!" says Claire. "Frank has explained that, even though becoming wealthy is a long-term process, it's completely achievable at our age. You have a couple more years to play with than me – if I can do it, you definitely can. Look at it like this, I have a business which theoretically puts me with an asset. But I'm no different to you at the moment. My business has essentially bought me a job. I should be able to create wealth from it, increase its value and the cashflow it generates but, right now, it doesn't work like that. Plus, I'm still renting – I haven't looked at buying somewhere since I broke up with Pete three years ago and moved out of his house. I feel even further away from my house-buying dream since paying for the funeral.

"Would you be interested in speaking to Frank? We could double-up on our meetings, so we don't take up too much of his time?"

Mark agrees and Claire emails Frank on Monday morning to explain her brother's predicament. Frank replies - he's happy to give it a go and asks Claire to share with him the Why she's created and the link for Mark to find out his own entrepreneur profile type online.

Chapter 7

Escaping the rat race

The first session with Frank and the brother and sister together begins with Mark's Big Reason. He wants to support his family, including his Mum, and make sure he and his wife can enjoy retirement. He would like the freedom to work closer to home or from another country if he and Sophie fancied a holiday. He wants to be a great Dad and do everything he can to make sure John would be proud of him – having the spare time to take over his Dad's role in FUNdraise would be a start. This particularly appeals to Mark as he was really close to his grandfather and supporting the veterans' associations would be a great way to honour his memory.

"OK, these can take a while to work out but once you've come up with a BIG reason, you start to find a way to make it happen. At the end of the day, it seems so simple, we call it a 'Blinding Flash of the Obvious,' meaning it joins up two previously unconnected piece of information. It's like switching on a lightbulb in your mind," explains Frank.

"Can you understand the importance of having a well-thought-out BIG reason, something that's bigger than you, bigger than just making a good living, and not just about the money and things we can buy with it?"

What Frank is about to say is relevant to both Claire and Mark because they both feel they are stuck in a job.

"If you were to rely on what you were able to generate from a salary alone, you'd limit your potential to the number of hours you have available to work multiplied by the amount of money you make hourly. What if you wanted to stop working or if for some reason you simply couldn't work? Your income would, in most cases, totally stop. Then, where would that leave you? You could work all your life, have a good pension and then die early like your Dad or you could create recurring income that not only sustains you in your lifetime but also supports your children too. This is why you need to commit to building wealth. Building a vision and creating wealth is a process you'll have to engage in over time - we're talking years, not months."

"How many years are we talking about here?" asks Mark. He's fed up of wasting time commuting and missing out on time with his kids.

"I'm hoping you'll like this Mark. To escape your job and the commute that goes with it, think of it as hitting the escape ESC key on your keyboard. ESC stands for Education, Support and Connection.

"Education means you need to take time to understand how the asset you're looking at really works. See if that asset fits in with your own entrepreneur profile and whether that's something you now want to explore. It's not a decision to act. It's a decision just to find out more, so you can then take the next step.

"The next step in the process is Support. Think about who will provide the education, when and whether they'll be providing independent guidance. The third step, Connection, means you connect or become connected to someone who's already putting in play the education that you've just started to learn about. It brings the education to life, so you can see if that asset is right for you.

"Creating wealth starts with learning, and the learning takes time. Once you make the decision to commit to wealth building, there's a natural, emotional response to try to get there quicker. This excitement is a real danger you must avoid. You must take time to learn, apply and benefit from real wealth strategies and principles - let wealth take its course.

"Bill Gates famously said that most people overestimate what they can do in one year and underestimate what they can do in 10 years. I've had some clients create wealth in five years but that doesn't mean the learning process stops.

"Clearly, Mark, one of the freedoms you will choose is time. Use your commute to plan your next steps."

Space:
Because the law of vacuum shows me everything grows to fill the available space, I need to create space for my wealth to grow.

"Building wealth is a long-term thing. It's a life-long approach, something that involves more than just learning a few strategies and ideas. It's more about changing your habits, changing the way you view life and the world from here on out. It's all about understanding the basic principles and applying them to everything you do during your life.

"There are steps involved in creating wealth. Escaping the rat race is a process, so you need a plan before you run in to work on Monday and hand your notice in! At first, almost all the income you generate is going to come from your job. The goal is to make enough and save enough to invest. Don't be in a hurry. Creating wealth is something you plan for - most people spend longer planning their holidays than they spend on their wealth plan!

"Think about which assets of the four you'd like to use to create wealth. Then before we move on to those in more detail, I want to share some more lessons on financial foundations with you."

Chapter 8

Identifying savings

This next step in education for Mark and Claire is on a video Frank likes to share in between coaching sessions. He knows Claire will make notes, but he wonders if Mark's learning style is similar. He emails the video link over to them.

Hi Both,

We've talked at length about mindset and now we start on the financial foundation principles. JFK famously said in his 1962 speech about the space programme, "The greater our knowledge increases, the greater our ignorance unfolds." He talked of "the hour of change and challenge, the decade of hope and fear, and the age of both knowledge and ignorance" and I think these statements carry forward for every person looking to reach their goals, whatever the time or place.

> As my knowledge, ability and capital grow, so does my ability to make bigger and better investment deals.

We want to grow your knowledge and getting to grips with your finances is an essential first step. This next piece of homework is a financial stocktake I recommend you do each year - please watch my video. It's important to emphasise that whilst this exercise focuses on saving you money, you should recognise that you cannot save your way to wealth - to do this you need to expand your knowledge and your means to invest in that expansion. Doing this exercise will reveal immediate savings which you can allocated to invest in your learning or to start building investments.

Take care, Frank.

Mark plans to watch the video on his next train ride back from the office but does not manage to get a seat – he could watch on his phone but will not be able to take notes. He saw Claire's notepad and decides he ought to write notes too – he is so used to typing at super-fast speeds, he will never take it in properly unless he hand writes them. Technology has the simple answer for now - he decides to take photos of each page of notes to store on the cloud until he has time to digest them and start his own notes.

Mark calls Claire to moan about his failed attempt at watching the video on his way back from work. They agree to watch it together, tomorrow after work. They plan to watch the whole way through and then go back to each section and discuss what they could save - two heads are better than one!

Cups of tea in hand, Claire and Mark settle down as she streams the video on to the larger screen in her living room. Frank's voiceover begins as he takes them through what each letter of DEBITS stands for and how it can help them review their own finances as they stand currently.

"In the foundation element, where we help you try to create wealth, we're looking really hard at what you already have in your financial life. And we begin that process with something we call debits - D.E.B.I.T.S. Each one of those letters stands for a part of your finances that we'll take a look at, to try and help you find money that you didn't realise was there. And when you discover that money, it's like plugging a leak. Then when you take that money and make it work, essentially you're creating money out of thin air."

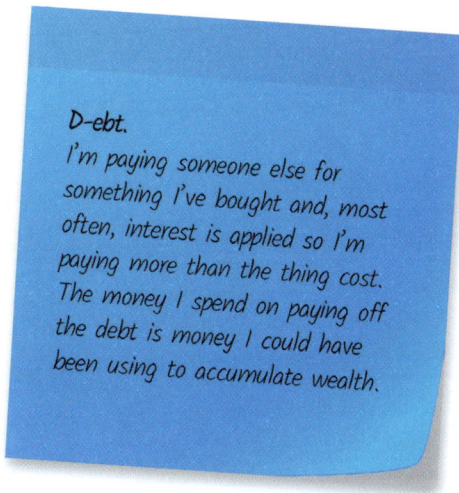

> D-ebt.
> I'm paying someone else for something I've bought and, most often, interest is applied so I'm paying more than the thing cost. The money I spend on paying off the debt is money I could have been using to accumulate wealth.

"The first letter D stands for Debt. And debt is a real challenge in life because you're paying someone else, and anything you spend on debt means the cost of what you've bought has gone up. This means that money is then going out of your life, which you can't use to accumulate wealth.

"First of all, let's think about consumer debt - credit card debt, personal loans, those sorts of things. Credit card debt is one people can easily understand - with the prevalence of credit cards, most people have got them. The high cost of debt is sucking money out of people's lives. If you can find the funds in DEBITS to repay your credit cards and completely eliminate them from your life, then you can start accumulating assets, not liabilities.

"The second aspect of debt most common to people is mortgages. The key here is to think about the ways you can reduce the overall cost of a mortgage. If you ever looked at a mortgage statement, on the last page it says, 'The total cost of this debt is X' and in most cases it's hundreds of thousands. So, anything that can focus your mind on reducing the overall cost of that debt will inevitably save you money, leading to the ability to build more wealth."

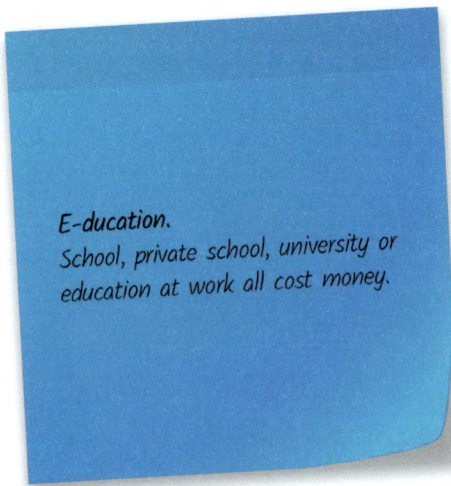

E-ducation.
School, private school, university or education at work all cost money.

"The second area that we want to focus on is E - Education. Now, it's true to say we're all aware that education costs money, whether it's learning through the education system - schools, colleges and universities - or education at work. Historically, the education system in the UK has not delivered practical business and wealth-building education. Just think back to the last time you went clothes shopping – I'm guessing if the sales person spoke to you at all, they asked you 'can I help you?' and you replied with something along the lines of 'no, thanks, I'm just looking.' Right?"

Mark and Claire nod their heads almost in unison.

"So, the business owner has learnt so little about business and selling, they're allowing their sales person to ask a question which almost always gets a negative answer and makes their prospects want to leave their shop! Now, think back to what you learned at school from the teachers about wealth building... yes, didn't think that'd take long! The point is you need to take the time now to get the education you need, so congratulations on taking this step.

"There are many ways you can participate in some education - books, podcasts and video programmes like this one can be a great, low-cost way for some people to learn. If that's all you need, then more of your money can be used to build assets. However, most people will need at least some human interaction to bring their learning to life, make it more personal to them and to keep them motivated, so they go on to achieve their medium and long-term goals. Be sure to do your research before you invest in that human interaction, so you find the right people for you, who are primarily driven by being on your side and helping you build wealth for yourself and are in a great position to help you do just that."

B-ills.

Do I know if my bills are all at the lowest, most competitive rate and do I actually need the thing related to that bill?

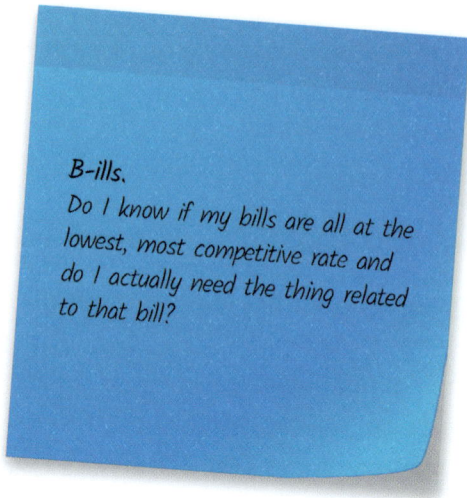

"Now the third area is B - Bills. We've all got bills, we know that. But isn't it often the case that we can take the bills we have to pay for granted? I encourage you to, at least once a year, get into the habit of looking at all your bills. Get your highlighter pen out and look for things that you don't really need any more, like a membership you're not using or a product or service you can get at lower cost.

"If you look at all the consumer websites available these days to reduce the cost of utilities and insurance, then you're in a much better place to be able to count the money you save. But then instead of just banking the saving, you must use that money for education, investing or debt elimination."

Claire stops the video. "Mark, if we're serious about this, we need to action these savings as we go. We'll watch it through like we said but then we should get the laptop out and start shopping for savings on the second viewing." Mark agrees and she presses play.

I-nsurance.
It's for those things that would be disastrous if you lost them. So, it's important to insure my life if I've got debt.

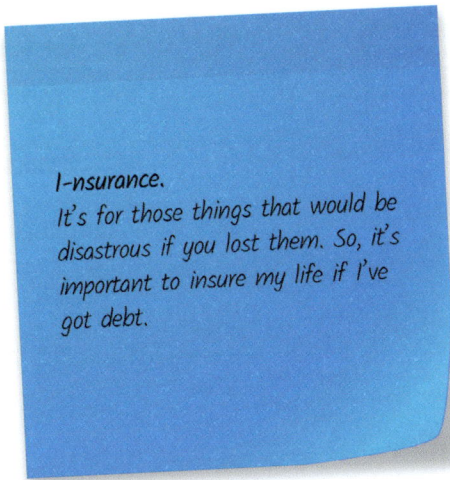

"Now, the I stands for Insurance. We all know insurance is important in life, but I want to stress to you how important it is for those things that would be disastrous if you lost them. So, it's important to insure your home, of course, and to insure your life, if you've got debt or dependents.

"And while I'm talking about life insurance, don't forget Relevant Life Cover. If you're a business owner or plan to be one, you get tax relief on Relevant Life Cover because the government want you to be a responsible business owner. That tax relief will reduce the premium. And if that reduces the premium, it puts more money in your life."

Claire also adds on her to-do list to find out more about how the government give tax relief on her life insurance as a business owner.

"Income protection insurance is also a high-priority insurance. If you fall ill, have an accident, are made unemployed or are otherwise unable to work, this will pay you a tax-free replacement income. Protecting your income in this way could prove vital, especially if you have family members whose wellbeing depends on the money you earn, or if you are self-employed and would not be able to keep up the cost of living on your own."

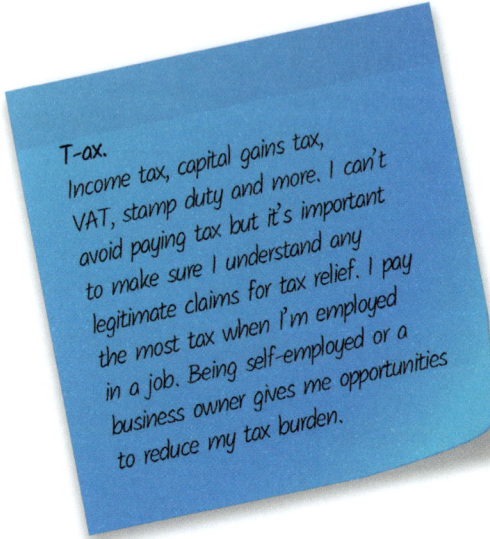

> T-ax.
> Income tax, capital gains tax, VAT, stamp duty and more. I can't avoid paying tax but it's important to make sure I understand any legitimate claims for tax relief. I pay the most tax when I'm employed in a job. Being self-employed or a business owner gives me opportunities to reduce my tax burden.

"The T for Tax affects us in every aspect of life and there's no escaping it. In fact, if you look online, an organisation called the Adam Smith Institute has something they produce every year called Tax Freedom Day. This is the day at which they calculate when the average person in the UK stops paying the taxes charged by the government and the money they earn is available to spend on themselves. And that day is normally around the end of May.

"That's why it's critical to work with tax experts as they should save you more than they cost."

S-upport costs.
When I'm paying somebody for taking a task off me. If I'm using someone like a broker for pensions and investments, make sure I'm getting value for money.

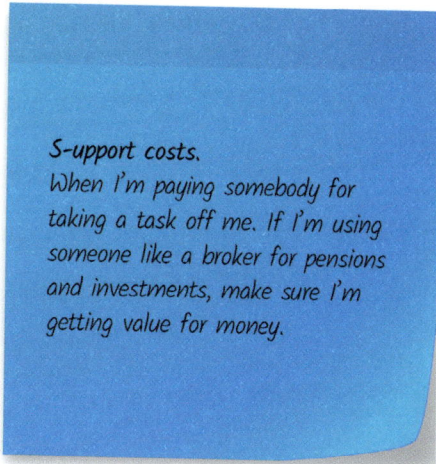

"And the final section in this foundation element of DEBITS is S for Support costs. Wherever you're building wealth already, I'm assuming you're paying somebody for the privilege of you delegating that task to them. And in my experience with investments or pensions, there are a number of people being paid. I'm not saying they shouldn't be paid, I'm saying you should make sure you get real value for money and, if possible, drive the costs of those services down. So for example, if you look at the variety of costs - IFA costs, costs of having the custodian, the wrapper, the box in which you're holding your investments in, fund manager costs - there are many ways you can buy low-cost tracker funds or even things known as ETFs or exchange-traded funds, where the cost of buying into investments is a fraction of the cost of paying for a fund manager.

"And if you've got an advisor, are you sure you're getting value? Have they plugged a siphon into your life and taken money out, or are they giving you value for money back? That's for you to determine with a regular checklist and process that will help you work out if you are getting value from the people you're delegating the task of helping you build your wealth.

"Remember, if you can reduce those costs, once again, that puts more money in your life for you to build wealth."

Mark has noted down the savings he needs to follow up:

Debt - mortgage. Paying £700 a month - will enquire with current mortgage provider and a comparison website to see if I can secure a better rate.

Bills - review the best deals on a comparison website to switch my utility bills - gas, electricity, phone / internet / tv

Insurance - life insurance is new but can look at home, contents, car, mobile phone on a comparison website.

Tax - don't think there's anything I can do on this?

Claire is enjoying this, it's almost like shopping but she could be saving money, not spending it! She notes down:

Debt - car loan and credit cards - review the results on a comparison website. I want to look at a more economical car so will do this before making changes to my car loan.

Bills - look at business utilities and supplier rates as well as personal bills - energy, courier, internet, phones. There are companies and comparison websites that can do some of this for me and find better savings

Insurance - business and personal insurances - car, buildings, contents.

Tax - meeting booked with accountant to review this.

Mark and Claire need to work through their DEBITS before the next session with Frank. They must reveal what savings they have made and what proportion of these savings they will allocate to investments and education. This education is going to help them create the assets they wish to build. With the cash saved for investments, they may buy Premium Bonds or even invest directly in the stock market themselves. They decide to make it easier; Mark will create a spreadsheet and share it on Google docs so they can openly discuss their situations. It will save time in their next meeting and begin a more open atmosphere for their family to discuss finances in the future.

Claire doesn't have any financial dependents, so she's made the decision she doesn't need life cover right now as she has no debt. However, she takes Frank's advice, making a simple will and arranges a Lasting Power of Attorney with Mark as her trusted person.

Mark's situation is different from his sister, he has a wife and young family who depend upon him and a mortgage to pay. This has been the wake-up call he needed. He had thought about getting a will in place after his Dad's funeral but now he can see how important it is to get it sorted, along with a Lasting Power of Attorney. He also checks in with his insurance broker. The life cover he has for him and his wife and the benefits from his employer are good enough for now, but he adds some income protection insurance and makes a note that he must review his life insurance if he ever leaves his job.

Chapter 9
Leverage, critical mass and learning

Frank is impressed with their progress and loves the thought process behind their DEBITS spreadsheet.

They've started work on saving money and have a totalizer on each of their sheets. Claire has saved the most, £462 a month so far, by changing from a petrol-fueled sports car to an electric car she lowered her car insurance, but the biggest saving was from Frank, introducing her to new government tax breaks on electric cars; that's also now a nice perk, Claire is offering her employees through the scheme and Baggins now has more room to ride along, so win:win:win! Mark's also made a great start. The exercise made him realise he was wasting £120 a year on insurance for his mobile phone, which was already covered by his joint bank account and his house contents' insurance premium. Once his mortgage review completes, he'll have clawed back £325 a month in total and he hopes to add to that by persuading his employer to adopt the electric car perk Frank recommended.

With each of them making an annual saving of over £3,000, they had a healthy start for their wealth development fund. They meet up with Frank who they hope will suggest some professional development and courses they could book on to, or authors and experts they can connect with, to maximise the learning from this fund.

"Those are fantastic savings, let's make good use of them - what will you do to increase your knowledge? Remember the E in DEBITS? You're on my coaching programme for free but in most cases, you have to invest in education. Let's continue our work together and the answer to where you invest your learning fund is likely to become clear to you. If you want some pointers after that, I'll be glad to help. For instance, you may find seminars or online learning courses you both want to sign up to and receive discounts for the second place.

"Now, it's time to move along with our financial foundation learning. I hope you're not running out of blue post-it notes yet Claire? I'm going to run through leverage with you before we look at what your next steps are."

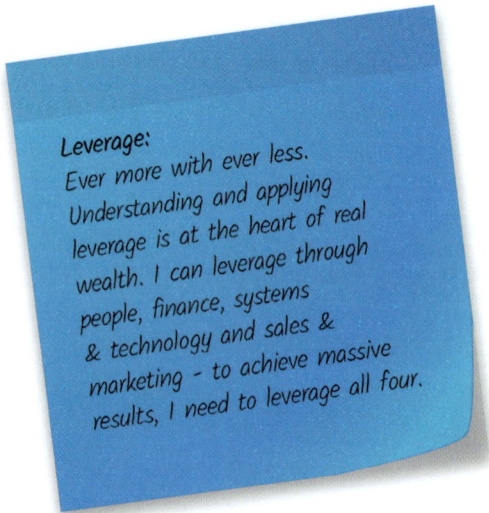

Leverage:
Ever more with ever less.
Understanding and applying leverage is at the heart of real wealth. I can leverage through people, finance, systems & technology and sales & marketing - to achieve massive results, I need to leverage all four.

"A great example would be leveraging a property investment using 25% as a deposit and taking on a mortgage of the remaining 75%. For example, if you have cash available of £100,000 and you were considering options on building your wealth, let me ask you a question: putting aside fees, if you went to a broker and asked to buy funds in the stock market, what is the value of the funds you could buy?"

Claire looks at Frank quizzically and says, "Well, £100,000, of course?"

"You're absolutely right," says Frank. "But, if you take the same £100,000 and leverage this with a mortgage of 75%, the same £100,000 gives you control of £400,000 worth of property. The rental income you would receive is based on the total value, not just the £100,000 and you can benefit from any increase in equity (the difference between what you owe on your mortgage and what your property is currently worth) to the tune of 4:1 as well!

"If the property increases in value by 30%, the equity in the property increases by 120% - illustrated with some simplified numbers:

£200k buy-to-let property bought with £50k cash and £150k mortgage

Value of property increases by £60k (30%)

The equity in the property increases from £50k to £110k = 120% increase

Critical Mass and Momentum:
The easiest way to think about
the law of critical mass is a steam
train – you need to pile on a lot
of coal to get the train moving,
but once the train is travelling
at a decent speed – the critical
mass point - then it's just a small
maintenance amount of coal to
keep it moving at that speed.

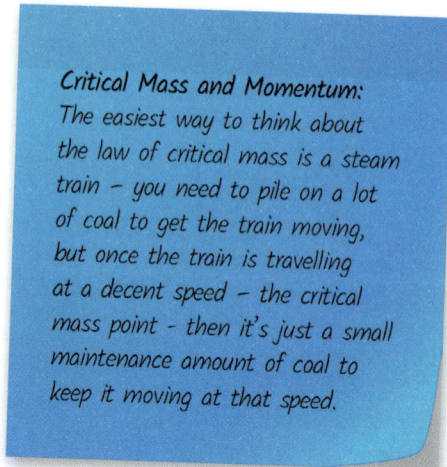

"Momentum is the distance before the train grinds to a halt if no more fuel is added. When you picture a lorry driver and a small car driver both travelling at the same speed and putting their vehicle into neutral, you can visualise how the lorry would take longer to reach a stop because of its greater weight. Equally, if the small car was travelling faster than the lorry, you can see how that could be enough to change the outcome.

"With a business, sales increase slowly initially while it's a case of adding one customer at a time, in a positive acceleration phase. Then sales increase rapidly, approaching an exponential growth rate when self-growth (self-perpetuation) kicks in, because it's not just new sales generated through your own marketing and sales efforts and investment, you also have repeat business from existing customers and new sales generated through referrals and word of mouth. Critical mass is also the size a company must maintain in order to sustain growth and efficiency.

"It took a lot of time and effort to sell the first few thousand mobile phones, but at the point of critical mass - around about 1997 - everyone started buying a mobile phone and sales shot up in a short period of time – acceptance of a product grows over time.

"It's your job as a business owner to grow the size of the business – so what exactly is the mass? It's the number of people who work in the business, the customers, the prospects and how many people know about us. And how do we grow mass in a business? Well, you can do that internally through getting better people, training, hiring more people and building better products and services; and externally through marketing, better sales approaches, more websites, more social media presence, more signage. Some of your marketing strategies will take a lot of time and effort before they produce sales. For instance, it could take years to build a strategic alliance, so it's important to balance long-term marketing strategies with short-term marketing strategies like direct selling.

"The critical mass point is when internal mass and external mass are strong enough to create a perpetually growing business. I believe the three keys for getting a business to critical mass are to work with someone like my business coach who understands how to build a successful business, applying leverage and allowing enough time to get there."

$$momentum = mass \times velocity$$

"In business, you could look at momentum as how long before customers stop buying from you if you stopped marketing, because the size (mass) of your business is driven by people and marketing (velocity)."

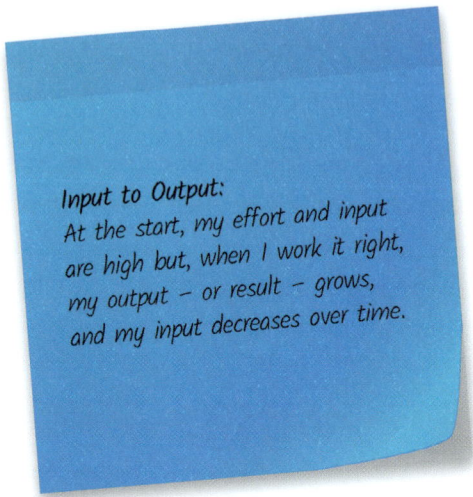

> **Input to Output:**
> At the start, my effort and input are high but, when I work it right, my output – or result – grows, and my input decreases over time.

"When you put the concepts of critical mass and momentum into wealth creation, it means you need to work hard creating and growing your wealth in the beginning. Then as time goes by, the amount of energy and effort needed to make each pound diminishes as the returns on what your energy and effort have created grow through 'compounding' – that's when you reinvest interest and capital gains from your assets to generate additional earnings, earnings on earnings if you like or to use a more technical term, exponential growth.

"There's a similar upward J-shaped curve with your learning – lots of time, work and learning before you execute a wealth-building strategy for the first time, then a much shorter time to learn some finer points to make the strategy deliver more the next time and the next time, until you've learnt all there is to know and just need to keep up to date with external changes like taxation and legislation."

If I do it right, at first, I make money. Then as I invest more and more, I transition from investing most of my time spent making money to most of my time spent managing money.

Divide to multiply:
Another way of looking at leverage is to divide to multiply. This mathematical formula for leverage helps me understand that for growth, I must divide so that I can multiply.

"If you multiply one by itself, all you get is one. There are many examples of dividing to multiply in life and in business. So, for instance, I might divide the process of making a sale into all the things that go into making that sale and then work out what I can do to increase the effectiveness of each step. Small improvements in the conversion rates from each step to the next step in the sales process can add up to a dramatic increase in sales – let's say you achieved a 5% increase in conversion rate for six steps of a sales process, well that multiplies through to a massive 34% increase in sales."

> **Get paid forever:**
> True leverage for me is about doing my work once and getting paid for it long-term or hopefully forever.

"A passive income is money you receive whether you work or not. Like income you receive from owning a successful business that you don't work in. Or royalty income you get from a book you only write once, or rental income from properties you own. It's the exact opposite of trading your time for money."

> **Value add or remove pain:**
> The only two reasons people will pay me in life are when I remove their pain (the more pain, the more I can charge) or when I add value to their life, asset or business.

"There are passive and active investments. If you're in business (an active investment), then two powerful wealth creation strategies are to add value and to remove pain. What do you think you could do at Florist Extras, Claire?"

"I suppose I'm already removing pain by delivering products to my clients, so they don't have to take time out of their business to pick them up? We add value with our packs to create the latest fashions in home decoration - like the door wreaths for Easter and Christmas," says Claire who is getting more confident with each coaching session.

"Good examples, Claire. As part of your work on your business this week, I'd like you to come up with three more ways you could add value for customers and three more ways you could take away their pain," says Frank. "Let's move on to the assets you've both committed to for your wealth building journey. Clearly, you're going for Business, but what else Claire?"

She explains she has her business and a pension and would like to add a property portfolio to the mix once she has secured a home first. Frank agrees that's a good start for her.

Mark had decided on one of his many commutes to work, he'd create a property portfolio for one of his assets to add to his ISA investment and pension. Frank is ready with his advice on building a property portfolio.

"Getting a good deal on a home you're willing to live in for a year or so while you fix it up is brilliant. In the meantime, you work and save, and then when the house you live in is ready, buy another fixer-upper and live in it, while renting the other one. You have an investment that's being paid for

75 percent by your tenants. Once your 75% mortgage is paid off - could be 20 years - you could get to keep 100% of the rent money as passive income, because your rental income is no longer needed to cover monthly mortgage repayments. Or you could choose to keep a portion of the rent money as passive income and use a portion of the rent money to cover a remortgage; the remortgage releases enough of the equity you've built up over time (the sum of how much you reduced your mortgage by with your monthly mortgage repayments + how much the value of your property increased in that time) for you to put down a cash deposit on another investment property, and so on."

Mark thinks he can go one better than this. A bit closer to town than where he lives with his family, the university is growing in popularity and the demand for good student accommodation is huge.

"I could combine a property portfolio of student houses and ensure my own kids have somewhere safe to live with their friends in a few years' time. I feel good about this idea as a father, as well as on a financial level. What do you think?"

"That's a fantastic idea Mark," says Frank. "You've attacked your wealth-building education and strategy so far. But there's one area of your financial foundation I want to cover before we finish today - pensions. It's not everyone's favourite subject, but it is important.

"The vast majority of people in the UK, like you two, have their pension money in the stock market and pay little attention to the fund; they're just trusting things will work out in the long run. A kind of buy-and-hope strategy. They simply leave that money invested until they hit retirement date, dealing with the pot they've accumulated at that point.

"Let's say the pot is worth £200,000 at age 65. They now need to turn that money into an income stream to live on. The traditional way of doing that is buying an annuity. This basically means you give the accumulated sum back to the insurance company and then they give you an income for the rest of your life, plus a pension for a spouse at, typically, 50% of the value if you pass away before they do. This is exactly what your Dad did. He got a pension for a while, then your Mum got a significantly reduced income after he died. And, of course, if you rely on getting a state pension, you'll find there won't be any significant pension benefits for you when you reach the seemingly ever-increasing state retirement age. This goes against the wealth principles of building a legacy you can be proud of, don't you think?"

Mark has struggled to come to terms with the difficult financial position his Mum was left in following his Dad's death. Between them, he and Claire have helped out as much as they can, "Dad clearly didn't appreciate the terms of his pension properly, but we're not going to make that mistake."

"It's good to hear," says Frank. "Delegating your money to a third party with no involvement is not a great idea. Not only can you never really assess the value of your pot but when you reach retirement, you have to work out how to draw money from it to live - known as drawdown. Now, if you pay little attention to how funds actually work in the build-up to retirement, how are you ever going to have the skills to manage the income? If you draw too much, you may run out of money in your latter years and live an existence of uncertainty and worry. That's why building wealth in multiple pillars makes sense, as opposed to purely relying on your pension to provide the lifestyle you want in your retirement.

"Most advisors in the UK calculate the likely drawdown they would recommend is around 4%. So, if you have £200,000 in the pot then this will generate £8,000 per annum. Can you see you would need a massive pot to be financially secure through just your pension? There's also stock market volatility to deal with. You're probably too young to remember the last crash but, when they happen, it's not unusual for pensioners to lose 30% or more of their total retirement funds in days, often leaving them no time to ever recover from the loss. So, the big lesson to take on board is to not rely solely on your pension. But that doesn't mean you can't make the most of it.

"I'm going to share a couple of things which will help you to take control of your pension."

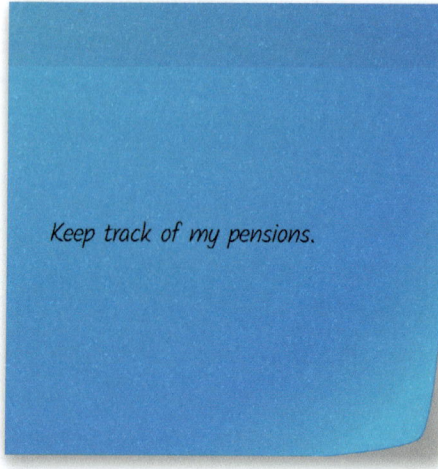

Keep track of my pensions.

"Did you know that billions of pounds' worth of pensions have been effectively lost, as people simply lose touch with and forget about their old private and workplace pensions. That's a huge sum of money that won't provide a future income or an inheritance to the people who deserve it. Over the years, through my business, we've helped hundreds of people track down these lost pensions and reunite them with the rightful owner. Are you sure you have a record of your pensions?"

Claire recently had a statement through for her private pension, "Yes, I only have one private pension and I know its current value."

Mark isn't quite as sure as his sister, "I have a pension with my current employer - I can login online to view the details. But I do remember working for a small tech firm quite a while ago, so I should look into what happened in terms of a pension there. I met Sophie while we were both working there, so she could be in the same situation."

"As I explained earlier, we're never able to control what happens in the stock market. But there are some things we can control, and one of those is charges," continues Frank.

Charges:
There are some things we can't control and some we can - charges is one I can control.

"Let's just say over the long term, when you take out the booms and bumps - any of the things that happen over which we have no control - the average gross return of the stock market is 6%. If we assume the fee charged by the industry is on average 2%, this means the net return over the long term will be 4% - the recommended pension drawdown for people at retirement.

"So, I want you to think about this in a different way. Would you sign a joint venture agreement with a partner where you put in all of the money and take all of the risk, but they take a third of the profit and have no accountability if you lose money?"

"But doesn't everybody just do that? Aren't fees just something we have to put up with?" asks Claire.

"Yes, in most cases you won't be able to avoid them completely but there are some actions that you can take to reduce them," says Frank

"No one will take better care of your money than you, and so I want to introduce you to the best-kept secret for entrepreneurs - the Director's Pension. If you want to take care of your money and, in this case, your pension, you'll need to understand the details behind this option. I'm going to take the time to explain this type of pension because it will likely be the sharpest tool in the toolbox on your road to wealth. The technical term for a Director's Pension is SSAS or Small Self Administered Scheme."

Claire laughs, "So not the armed forces' SAS then?"

"No," says Frank. "And not to be confused with SaaS - software as a service - either. A SSAS pension can help you build multiple streams of wealth, building recurring income both inside and outside of your business. Whether it's a trading business like yours Claire or a property business like you intend to build Mark. Having a SSAS is like turning your pension into a business. The Inland Revenue allow business owners to take complete control of the pension funds and, in doing so, the directors become trustees of their own funds - critical for control."

"So, only directors can have them?" asks Mark, who hasn't set up a company yet.

"That's right. A business has directors and a SSAS pension has trustees. A business strives to make profits, on which they pay tax, and a SSAS generates profits which are tax free. A business uses an accountant to file the accounts once a year and a SSAS uses a professional administrator to file the accounts to ensure the scheme remains tax free. So, if you can run a business, you can operate a SSAS and the benefits are massive for you, your business and your family."

Clare and Mark have perked up somewhat since Frank first started talking about pensions.

Frank smiles, "I've seen that spark of interest before. We've had literally thousands of business owners learn about SSAS, showing them how to build a huge tax-free pot. It's a bit like a family trust fund to support the business or to build assets to diversify, making the business owner safer from the tide of uncertainty that affects us all. The pension is essentially ring fenced from the business and can't be touched by creditors.

"As a SSAS trustee, you can take complete control of your investments. Let me give you a few examples of what some of our savvy business owners, who have followed my wealth building programme, have done once they get the control of their pension. First off, you can invest in buying your own business premises, so you pay rent to yourself and not a landlord."

"Wow!" exclaims Claire. "I'd much rather own my warehouse than be shelling out money every month for somebody else to get wealthy on."

"I thought that benefit would be appeal to you," continues Frank. "You can also support the business in other ways, such as buying your own company shares to increase liquidity or even lend money from the pension to the company when it needs funds. No other type of pension can do this - not a private pension like you have or a Self-Invested Personal Pension. Now, there are rules, as you'd expect, but my team can give you professional advice when you're ready to start your SSAS."

"Is there anything I can do in the meantime while I don't have business premises?" asks Mark.

"Sure," says Frank. "Many of my clients like property and they can use their SSAS to build a portfolio of commercial property to create ongoing rental income. Others use them to facilitate the purchase of commercial property, like shops with flats above, separating the ownership so the pension owns the commercial unit and you or your business can own the residential part - we call this strategy 'shops with tops'! Some of my clients become property developers, buying old offices and converting them into apartments for sale. Don't get me wrong, any business or property actions will need careful consideration, sound education and robust due diligence, but I hope you get the picture? There's so much more to pensions than meets the eye."

Claire hazards an idea, "I might even be tempted to pay money into my pension knowing it can help me and my business?"

"Yes," says Frank. "Any contributions you make will qualify for tax relief so, basically, you get the corporation tax back. How's that for leverage? Plus any profits are free of corporation tax, capital gains tax and inheritance tax.

"Finally, you can have up to 11 members in a SSAS. Mark, you can add your spouse and kids in the future, so it's like having a growing tax-free trust fund for the family. Or you two could collaborate -we have many siblings who have set up and run their SSAS pension together.

"We'll revisit this once you have taken care of your wealth foundation. Meanwhile, let's get a proper stock take of all the pensions you have first."

They both nod enthusiastically and resolve to get on the task straight away.

"We know your Dad didn't leave the world in the best financial position but the way you two are going, you'll be able to execute a good legacy – maybe even something in John's memory?"

Both Claire and Mark now have a good idea of where some of their learning fund needs to go - property and business expertise.

Chapter 10

A business masterclass

Frank is off enjoying a rugby sevens tournament in Hong Kong. He calls Claire on Skype. He says, "I'm not saying this because I want to disappear off to watch the rugby but when I spoke about bringing in the experts for certain areas of your wealth creation, I meant it.

"You'd hire a personal trainer for fitness, a dietitian for nutrition and you've been working with me to learn about building wealth. Now, I think it's time you took on a world-class business coach to make more headway with your business – it's your main asset where you intend to increase value.

"I want to introduce you to a great business coach who can take you through the practical steps for working ON your business rather than IN it. But before I do, I want to share with you some insights into business which are critical. Most business owners, Claire, don't get massive value for all their blood, sweat and tears. You know this from your Dad's experience when he hastily sold his flower shops.

"The sad fact is that the vast majority of business owners don't have a solid exit plan and as the business revenues and processes depend so much on them as owners, there's very little for them to sell. Yet we know, in the end, all business owners will inevitably exit their business. What's tragic is the date of their exit is out of their control and catches them so often by surprise. It could be a business issue like a major disruption to their industry or an over reliance on a supplier or one major customer. The sad state of the high street shows us how uncertain business life can be. Other reasons can be more of a personal nature, like an unexpected breakdown in a relationship, a health issue for them or a loved one or, sadly, the death of the owner. All of these affect the business value and the legacy for those left behind.

"To give you the best chance to get the highest possible value for your business, I want you to keep two fundamental principles in mind as you work with your business coach. Firstly, find ways to create recurring revenue in your business so you are not starting each month from zero. There are so many benefits to this. Your business will be more predictable, your cashflow will be healthier and you'll be able to increase your own safety. If you never sell the business, you can draw this repeatable income in the future. If you do choose to sell, your business will be more attractive to buyers, securing a higher multiple on exit.

"Secondly, find ways to make the business less dependent on you personally. Create documented systems and processes as you go and train others to operate them. This will also serve you well whether you sell or keep the business in the long term.

"It's not going to be easy but the business coach I'm referring will guide you, make you accountable and keep you on track. I'll check in again with you soon."

Frank introduces Claire to his business coach, James, via email and they set up their first meeting at his office in

Birmingham. She explains her situation and the progress she's made in goals and mindset through her work with Frank. She's excited to take control of her business and make it work for her, rather than feeling a slave to it. She explains how she feels very close to her brother's situation of being an employee, rather than a business owner.

James starts the first day of his fortnightly business growth coaching with Claire and she starts a new notepad.

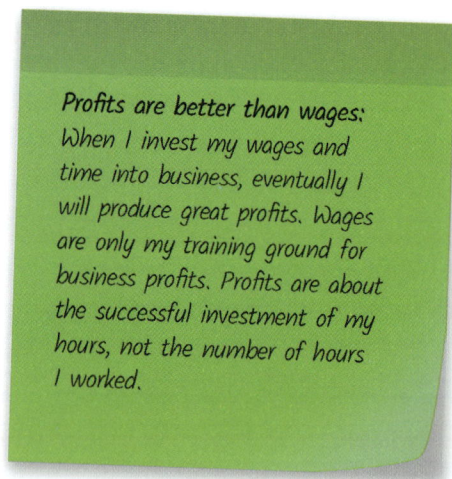

> *Profits are better than wages:* When I invest my wages and time into business, eventually I will produce great profits. Wages are only my training ground for business profits. Profits are about the successful investment of my hours, not the number of hours I worked.

James begins, "If you want to create great wealth, you invariably will find that it will happen as a result of being in business for yourself. This is for a number of reasons; you can leverage through people, finance, systems, technology, and marketing, plus the taxation system favours business owners.

"When you're an employee, the first thing that happens as soon as you are paid is that tax is taken off. You never get to see your gross pay, do you? So, whatever you need to buy has to come out of your post-tax earnings; from whatever is left over after the tax man has taken his share. But when you're a business owner, most of what you need to buy comes out of money before it is taxed. The tax man only helps himself to a share of whatever is left over after all your spending on the business is done."

> *Return on investment (ROI):*
> *Better than profits, because when I reinvest my profits, I can multiply my returns. Profits are my training ground for ROI. My ROI is about the successful investment of my money, not my time.*

"Remember, our most valuable asset is our time – once it runs out, it can't be replenished. Most employees end up time poor. And so far, you've essentially bought yourself several jobs in your business. Through owning a business, you generate cashflow by way of profits. Cashflow is usually passive in nature; it keeps coming whether you get out of bed or not. Of course, it all depends on having a business that can run profitably without you.

"The trick is to learn - to follow what others have done successfully before you. There is no need to reinvent the wheel, so why try? The one thing you've decided is to grow this business and use it as an asset. It's a good thing because Frank will tell you, business ownership is needed to create ultimate wealth. Some of what I'm going to run through now will help your brother too."

Employee:
Most people think this is about earning as much as you can, but they're wrong. If financial freedom is my goal, I need to think of this as being paid to learn. Learn as much as I can.

"The whole point of having a job during the early stage of any career is so you can learn, not just earn. Sure, the salary is nice, but don't let that mask the real reason why you have the job - that is to learn as much as you can, while you can."

Manager:
Now I've learned the skill of my job. It's time to learn to manage a group of people and resources so the job gets done and the goals are achieved without doing it myself. It's another level of learning on my growth path.

"Getting to grips with the 'people dynamic' is something that's invaluable in becoming a good manager, and eventually a great leader. Leadership will enable you to use the principle of leverage to its utmost. Most business owners are still oblivious to the power of leverage because they've spent most of their working time learning their trade or profession rather than the business of business."

Leader:
Now I know how to manage the resources, it's time to learn how to lead the people and get the team to come together to achieve amazing results. Leading is the next level of my learning after managing.

The first step to owning a business is often through a multi-level business where people recruit others to sell products or services in a sort of 'tiered' level. Claire thinks about some of these she's seen her friends get involved with, beauty and wellness brands always caught her eye.

Network marketing business:
Often, the first step into my own business is through multi-level business where I have the products and systems provided to me. I just have to learn how to run my own business and, more importantly, how to motivate, recruit, market and sell.

"The multi-level marketing business runs on two levels. There's the obvious level where you earn an income from the product you sell and there's the not-so-obvious where you earn a commission from everything those you recruit under you sell. And it's here where you can earn the most. The more people you have under you, the greater your earning potential – and this form of income is all passive."

Part-time business:
It's the step before I go out on my own, and a favourite choice for tradespeople and consultant types, whereby they do work on the side. Multi-level marketing and part-time businesses can lead to amazing futures.

"These businesses are usually started by people while they still have regular jobs. Not everyone has the ability to raise enough funds to get a new business going or the courage and confidence to give up their main income, so they ease into it rather more casually. They get going gently, building up their customer base and an income while they have a job until they reach the point where the business is viable enough for them to quit and work full time in the new business. You now become self-employed."

Self-employed:
Now I've made the step. There's a great deal to learn and master. As I grow, so will the business. This is the hardest step. I need to stick with it and remember my first business or two will be more about learning than earning.

"Karma is the basic Universal Law that says every action has a reaction. Or every result has a cause. It is one of the basic laws of business too. So, how does it apply to the self-employed person? To achieve a certain result in your business - say a turnover of £5,000 in your first month - then you need to take some action to make it happen. If you take no action at all during your first week other than to organise your office, set up the filing cabinets, arrange your phone account and email address, then how can you expect to make any sales? You'd expect instead to make zero money because you took zero income-earning action."

In any business, there are two types of activities I need to undertake: Production activity and income-generating activity. Everything to do with my office, factory, stock, and staff are called production activity. Marketing, sales, and client delivery are income-generating activities. I need the former but I also need the latter.

> **Manage my own business:**
> Now I've grown the business and employed people - instead of managing it as the sole employee of my business, I now have other people to recruit, remunerate and manage. So much to learn, and I still have to do my work 'in' the business.

"You'll most probably find it hard to 'let go' of some of the tasks you previously did. But you will have to, or you run the risk of losing your first employee. You need to get used to the idea that someone else can be as good or better at doing some things than you are. After all, why else would you have hired them? If you're the superhero continually stepping in to save the day, your team members won't grow to their potential and you won't ever have a business that works so you don't have to."

> **Leading my own business:**
> I've gone from working 'in' to working 'on' the business and my years of learning and hard work are starting to pay off.

"Working *in* the business has to do with *doing* the work of the business. So, for example, if we were talking about a hairdressing salon, the owner would be working *in* the business when they are cutting hair. They would be working *on* the business when they are involved in managing the business and doing activities such as planning, budgeting, setting in place marketing strategies, hiring, and training hairdressers to be as good or better than themselves.

"I'm still stunned that most business owners don't know of the biggest business secret there is. I'm excited by the power of this to multiply your profits. Through our team and organisation, I literally have access to dozens of proven strategies within each of the five ways to grow your profits and also within each of the four ways to make your business work, so you don't have to. I'm going to pick out a handful of strategies from each area over the next couple of weeks which I believe are best suited to grow your business, but I'll need your input and inside knowledge to prioritise. That'll then form the framework for our first year of working together and we'll repeat the process of building our action plan each year. This is going to be huge. For instance, you've shared with me you're currently using one or two lead generation strategies. Well, we've now got access to over 100 strategies to increase your leads. If you apply just a couple more powerful lead-generation strategies, what's that going to do to your number of leads, sales, and gross profit? The key is to add one or two business growth strategies to your business each month, so compounding kicks in for your profit growth.

"The leader will then begin reaping the rewards that come from more profits and a well-trained, motivated and organised team in place – this is usually where they begin to receive some form of passive income from the business."

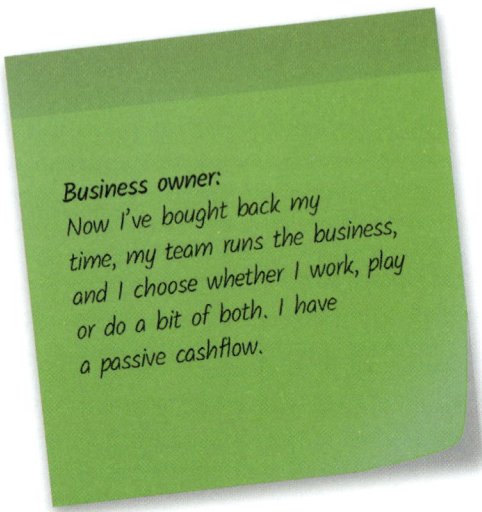

Business owner:
Now I've bought back my time, my team runs the business, and I choose whether I work, play or do a bit of both. I have a passive cashflow.

James was right, her brother would definitely benefit from some of this, so they arrange a catch-up at their favourite café.

Chapter 11

A property priority

Once Claire has told Mark about her business coaching sessions with James, he fills her in on his progress. He's made a start on his property journey. His education has taken him further into the multi-let student accommodation strategy. Since their last meeting Frank has hooked Mark up with a property expert – Mark now has a mentor. Frank's ESCape key method is working and his learning has accelerated his progress.

"Soph told me the other day that she's so proud of the positive direction we've taken from the tricky situation we found Mum in after Dad died. I've got a fire in my belly again and it's been nice to learn something other than IT developments for once. One thing we have to get our heads round is how not all debt is bad debt."

Mark pulls out his notes for Claire to see. She certainly hasn't written off a property portfolio as an asset she could build in the future, so she takes the time to write down Mark's notes in her own journal for then.

Good debt is good:
I enjoy debt when my debt is
paid for by someone else or one
of my investments, but
- a large mortgage for an
  expensive home
- car loan for a nice-looking car
- credit cards to pay for holidays
  and finance for sofas etc...
destroys wealth and is
bad debt.

Property is a multi-faceted strategy.

Frank explained to Mark that there are many ways to build wealth in property and that this investment type is one of the best for following a proven formula, which would suit Mark. The entrepreneur profiling tool sent to him when he first started on his wealth-building journey revealed he was a detailed and diligent personality type. He was most likely to enjoy following processes and Mark felt certain this path would play to his natural strengths.

"Frank gave me a book on various property strategies and encouraged me to do some research on the figures on the income for single buy-to-let and multi-let properties to compare the pros and cons. It's incredibly interesting. I've even created a program to run the numbers for me so I can easily evaluate purchase values and rental incomes.

"I calculated the return on renting a house or flat to a family would be around 4-6% and provide a gross income per property of around £500 per month. I decided that way would take too long to build the wealth I need to be able to give up my job. I'm pleased because it convinced me that my multi-let strategy is where I wanted to go."

Frank had connected Mark to two of his clients, one who had a portfolio of multi-let properties where he was charging rent by the room to young professionals.

"I visited one of the properties. All the bedrooms were ensuite and the communal areas were high spec with loads of fridge and cooking space. The average rent they were charging was double that of a single let. They do occasionally have a room vacant but that's never as bad as having a whole property empty. Going down this route, I'd have to prepare myself for more tenant contact during the year - you're likely to get a higher turnover of tenants because you're dealing with more people with changing circumstances.

"Frank's other client specialised in student property surrounding Manchester's university campuses. Frank said he'd got clients who specialised in providing rooms for young doctors, veterinary students, agricultural colleges, and others concentrate on short-term lets to tourists. I'm loving the sheer diversity of investing in property!

"But I'm favouring the student model for a few reasons. Firstly, while I still have my job, I can focus on the student intake at the same time each year. There should be minimal disruption because they'll sign up from September for the full academic year, then we'll have a couple of months in the summer to prepare for the next intake. I've also found out I can arrange a rental contract where the payment of the rent is guaranteed by the students' parents, reducing the risk enough for me to get things underway with my new property mentor, Fiona."

A property has potential for capital appreciation but, remember, in wealth building, cashflow is king.

I may get a 4-6% yield on a typical buy-to-let investment. I could double this if I convert the property to a multi-let.

"There's definitely an opportunity to get involved with commercial property or even property conversions in the future but I'll keep that on the backburner for now."

I can create value by converting commercial properties. If I learn the skills, these projects could treble my investment.

With the help of a mortgage broker, recommended by Fiona, Mark has acquired two properties in quick succession.

"Sophie's agreed to re-mortgage the house to fund the first properties. It's a long-term plan but it'll make a huge difference to our future. She's finally back nursing full-time but, ideally, we'd like to get to the point where she can choose whether she'd like to go part-time, work some hours with me or start something up of her own. One thing's for sure, she's got some great ideas to help make sure these student digs strike a balance between my preference of economical budget-style and her focus that they need to be attractive to parents and their kids. She has a strong view on what would be acceptable for our kids when they leave home and I think it's only going to be a positive thing to get a reputation as a student landlord of choice."

Based on the numbers Mark has run on his program, he thinks he'll be able to reduce the time on his day job within just a few months of having his first intake of student tenants.

"I've also started going to some local networking events. I'm curious to see if other property investors use anything like my program and if I can bring any of my IT skills to the wider property community. I've got a few ideas brewing!"

Chapter 12
Control and momentum

Claire emails Frank with a quick update:

Dear Frank,

It's been 18 months since we started working with you. Mark has four properties in his portfolio and is on the lookout for his next, and my business is going well with my profits growing and my team taking on more responsibilities.

I think it might be time to get bigger premises but I'm not sure how best to finance it? Is now the time to sort out my SSAS pension?

All the best,

Claire

Frank loved how Claire was thinking. He knew she had a private pension that she'd not paid much attention to since she'd received the last annual statement.

Hi Claire,

Glad to hear things are progressing nicely!

You're right. Using a SSAS, you could explore moving into a bigger warehouse or buy and extend the existing one, if the landlord is amenable. I know you have your private pension and, from what you've said, you have a sizeable sum in your business bank account. You could consider making a tax efficient lump sum contribution to make the pot big enough. Any rent would be paid by the business directly into your SSAS. That will build a bigger pot for you independent of your business and also keep the property ring fenced and secure for you too. Remember, I said that the SSAS can help you and your business. You should definitely explore this.

You should also speak to Mark about the possibility of collaborating - you could pool your pensions if you felt this was the right thing to do. It's a property strategy worth considering.

I'll put you in touch with one of my trusted advisors who can help you assess how to fuel your SSAS. Meanwhile, take a look at the video attached which explains more details about SSAS pensions, the HMRC approval process and how to operate a SSAS with the help of a professional administrator.

All the best,

Frank

> **SSAS:**
> I can create a SSAS that helps my future and that of my business. I am the Trustee in charge and the master of its success. I can collaborate with others. This is so empowering!

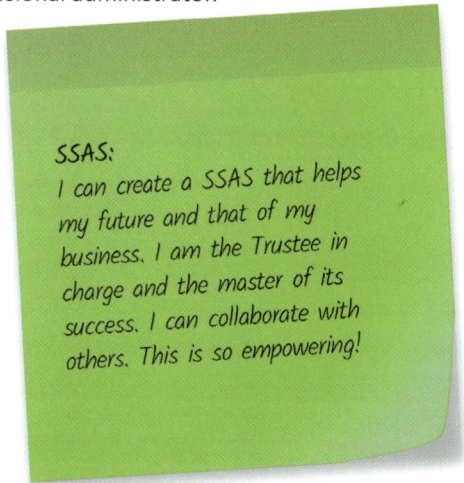

Claire forwards on the email from Frank to Mark. They chat about the possibility of collaborating on a SSAS. Claire has enough funds to buy a better warehouse and office for her business having arranged the transfer of the funds from her private pension and the lump sum from her company. But they both decide they don't want to complicate the decisions of her floral sundries business with Mark's pensions.

"It's been a worthwhile discussion though," says Mark. "I wouldn't rule out collaborating in the future - maybe on a different property project? I know that's something you definitely want to look at for yourself, sis. Now I've got these four properties, I'm generating some good recurring income. The security of that gave me the confidence to ask work if I can do more hours from home, knowing if they said no, I could probably manage without the job entirely. As it is, I've almost completely eliminated that awful daily grind of commuting. I've got so much more time to spend with Soph and the kids. I'm doing the morning school run and the kids' karate class on Thursday evenings - I could never have done that before. I feel like the momentum is picking up."

It's not long until their next meeting with Frank is scheduled. Frank thinks it's time to get more in to the nitty gritty of the power of leverage and sends the pair a video to watch before the meeting. Claire brings her wealth coaching notepad out from her desk drawer, the one reserved for her latest professional development journal and the post-it notes she saves for her time with Frank and James. She hits play on the latest video Frank has shared.

Compounding – time and rate:
Leverage uses the effect of compounding. The higher the percentage rate and the longer the time, the better the leverage.

"If you want to start investing, you need to research what will give you the best return based on the two elements of compounding - time and rate."

Critical mass:
Compounding and leverage bring me to a point of growth known as "critical mass". Where I have already done all the work and the results just keep growing and self-perpetuating.

Momentum:
I need to remember that to get wealth growing or a train moving, it takes massive effort at the start, but once it's running, I just need to tend the fires.

Grow or die:
A tree can never stop growing and just stand still. It's either growing or dying. So is my cashflow, capital and, ultimately, myself and my wealth.

Frank gives a great example of this as he rounds off the video.

"By just standing still and not growing in value, the ten-pound note would be losing value simply because of devaluation. But there is, or could be, more to it than that because the economy is growing all the time and this makes the value of the ten-pound note even worse, comparatively speaking. It turns out that hoarding cash under your bed is not a recommended wealth strategy! Similarly, in business if sales stand still, overheads will continue to grow and with time the losses kill the business. With product development, if innovation stops, in time a competitor comes up with a better product and sales decline to the point where the business is no longer viable."

Claire packs away her notepad and decides to take Baggins for a walk to spend some time reflecting on the latest lessons. Getting out in the fresh air on a dog walk has always been one of her favourite ways to unwind but more recently it has also given her the space to formulate new ideas for her business.

Chapter 13
Creating capital

It has been four years since John's funeral, and it feels like a lifetime since Frank saw his friend. The one consolation is the change he's seen in Mark and Claire. He sees they have the potential to stretch their goals and schedules just half an hour with them over Skype.

After the pleasantries, he gets down to business and says, "Massive action always leads to massive results. Let's review your progress - where have your efforts taken you and how do we maximise the results for the future? Here's more for your notebooks.

"Up until now, I've encouraged you to create cashflow because the recurring nature of this is the essence of wealth. But to turbo charge your success and to add further layers of compounding, I want to discuss with you the extra dimension of creating capital and there are a number of ways to do this. It's by combining large inflows of capital and predictable cashflow that you'll be taken from financial independence to financial abundance. When you're at the level of abundance, you can create a more powerful impact for your family, your community and the causes you care about."

> **Create capital:**
> Eventually, I will have learned
> enough to start to put deals
> together for others to be part
> of, always keeping a percentage
> for myself.

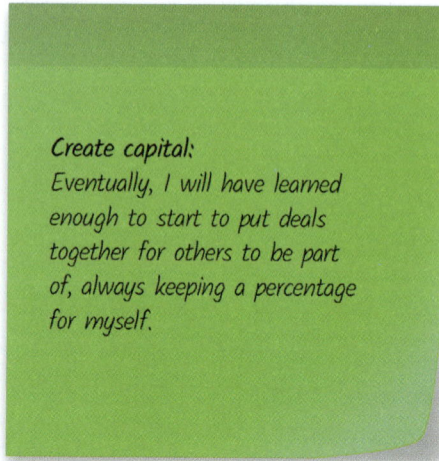

"So, how are things going for the both of you?"

Claire starts, "Thanks to the support from James, my business coach extraordinaire, my business is systemised with a great team, consistent cashflow, powerful marketing and multiple sales channels - an online retail platform, a craft community, Amazon and eBay - and increased profits.

"I've begun to explore ideas that will create recurring income in the business and because my team is capable of running the main part of it, I've been able to take more time off for myself. I love big nature, so when I can book my favourite dog sitter to look after Baggins, I've had a few lengthy holidays in South Africa, Canada and even snuck in a last-minute deal to Iceland - all without the stress and guilt I used to feel whenever I took a break. It's great because I come back rejuvenated, recharged and ready to explore new ideas. I'm firmly keeping in mind your lessons of creating recurring income and reducing the reliance of the business on me - I use it as my compass when working with James.

"One thing I've done is pull together a book of craft activities combining our product packs with easy how-to guides to keep the kids busy during the school holidays. I know how Sophie is so keen to cut down the kids' screen time and so we ran a focus group to look at what crafts should make it into the book. We ran a social media campaign using high-profile influencers in the parent space, sharing stories about the craft packs and book. Alongside that, we had online advertising and a PR campaign. The sales of the craft book show how I can create something once and get paid for it over and over again, plus a book sale regularly goes hand-in-hand with buying one of our craft packs from Amazon.

"The focus groups threw up something else which surprised me. We discovered the silk flowers we use in some of the craft packs have a truly calming effect on kids and the fact they are allergy-free has proved popular with special needs kids. I never thought a simple idea like this would end up being so truly rewarding.

"But that's not the biggest breakthrough the business has had this year. Do you remember why I chose the floral sundries business rather than fresh flowers like Dad's business? I was always troubled by the wastage with fresh produce and, back in January, I visited one of my prospective customers who specialises in floral arrangements for the hospitality industry. They'd been looking for a solution to provide longer-lasting arrangements for outdoor events, so I showed them how they could create beautiful alternatives using our silk and dried flowers, sometimes combined with fresh blooms for a dramatic effect. Since they've trialled my products, their customers have raved about them, so I pitched the idea to a company offering a fresh flower subscription service. They deliver fresh flowers to businesses and agreed to a joint venture to bring in my products. It's opened up the service to a wider market as some businesses are willing to subscribe where they wouldn't before because the arrangements last longer than the fresh flowers. The initial results are good, we've got a growing rate of subscriptions making healthy profit margins, so we're excited about the future."

Frank listens to Claire's summary and smiles, "You've come a long way Claire. I'm delighted you have the systems and team in place to allow you to be a leader of the business, taking it to the next level. There's even more to come.

"How are you doing with your property business Mark?"

It's Mark's turn and he's proud to share his progress, "I've got six student properties and last week I had an offer accepted on the seventh. What I've enjoyed is systemising the business. I've created a complete process for every aspect - from detailed specifications on kitchens worktops, bathrooms, and appliances to lighting and decor - into a fool-proof system for my team to follow.

"We ended up calling our tenants 'housemates' because Soph thought it would appeal to them in our marketing and perhaps even build a bond with our team, minimising the number of mishaps you get in student accommodation! She designed a welcome pack of toiletries and she's loved thinking of the extra touches she'd like to see if our two kids were away from home. We're even using Claire's silk flower arrangements in the communal areas - they seem to be going down especially well at the end of each term when we let the housemates take them home for their Mums!

"The marketing and sales processes work well but that's down to our reputation as a landlord. Our attention to detail means the properties are always snapped up and the income flows in nicely. Having the team in place is a godsend - it would be time consuming if I didn't. I remember you saying, Frank, a business must be able to work without you. I wouldn't want to get sucked back into work and miss out on the family time I've got used to.

"Of course, I still use my IT skills. I created an online app to help my team smoothly transition the properties from one university year to the next. The app allows them to record the inventory and inspect the properties with a photographic record. Then our housemates and their parents have a simple interface to login to. We never seem to have any disputes.

"Now I've been able to give up my IT job completely, I'm considering taking my property business to the next level. To be more tax efficient, I created JS Properties. I'm proud to be able to name the business after Dad - John Spencer Properties. I've even had some of my business associates and other landlords asking whether they can use my systems."

Frank is impressed - he's not surprised to see Mark's entrepreneur profile was really accurate. His recurring income is enough for him to be free from relying on a salaried job, while his team and systems seemed to be working well.

His students had excelled themselves. But he knew they could go further.

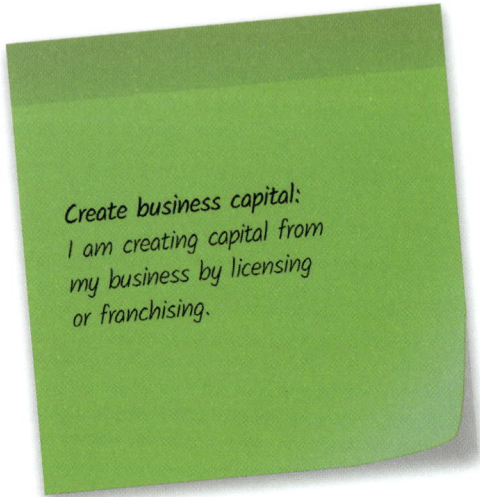

Create business capital:
I am creating capital from
my business by licensing
or franchising.

"The reason this is so rewarding is because you only have to do the work of building your business once, systemising it once, and then selling it forever. This is a great way to create business capital.

"Claire, you've done a great job so far. As you've created predictable income and robust business systems, you're ready to explore the idea of creating real value from your efforts. In effect, you've created intellectual property, often simply called IP. One of the best ways to capitalise on your IP is to allow others to use it under a licence or franchise arrangement. The beauty of this is you're able to charge a capital sum for it and generate an ongoing royalty income as well. The book can go so far and will add to your credibility, but the franchise is potentially much more rewarding for you and for potential franchisees too. While a franchise is not for everyone, of course, the benefit to the franchisee is the systems and support reduce their chance of failure and they are willing to pay a premium for that. I'll connect you with some of my clients who have a successful franchise model for you to learn more.

"This next lesson is clearly aimed at Mark and his progress, but I know you're interested in property as a future investment asset Claire," says Frank.

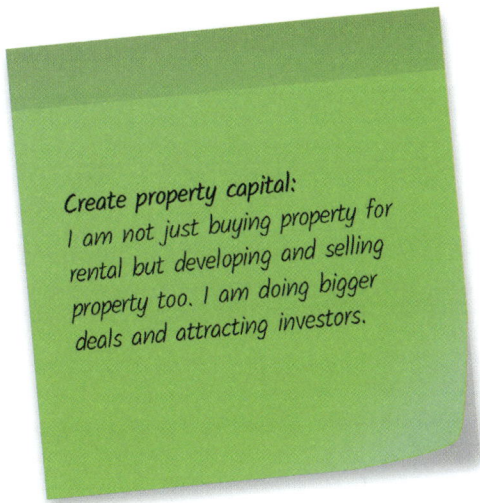

Create property capital:
I am not just buying property for rental but developing and selling property too. I am doing bigger deals and attracting investors.

"Mark, likewise, you've done an outstanding job too, using a different asset. You can take things to a higher level as well. As we know, property is an expensive asset and even using leverage, your portfolio size will depend on the amount of capital you have available.

"Remember, you have capital in your pension. Do you remember the concept of the SSAS pension Claire used so well to buy her business premises? You could use your pension capital for property of a different type to your student homes. You could use the funds to acquire commercial property, turning it into residential property like apartments or houses for sale.

"If you wanted to learn how to do this from the experts, you could use the facility in a SSAS to lend to others who operate this model successfully. Then you can see, at first hand, how it works, what the risks and rewards are, and decide if it's the right course for you to follow. If you're interested, I can make a suitable introduction for you.

"You also have the option of attracting inward investment into your student homes model. With people noticing your business and being impressed with the growth and systems, you can share your IP as part of the deal."

Mark has mixed feelings, "I'd be nervous about bringing in other investors. What if they wanted to make changes to a system I'm happy operating? But then, on the other hand, they could offer advice to make my systems better and more profitable. I think I've just talked myself into seriously considering the option."

"And through the good name you've created for yourself, you may find investors who are simply looking for an expert to provide a good return on their investment with little involvement in the project," adds Frank.

Once again, the wealth coach has given Claire and Mark the inspiration to stretch their goals.

Chapter 14
Investments for the future

Over the next 12 months, Claire and Mark take these ideas forward - Claire with franchising and Mark with larger property deals.

The systems in place for Claire's business have made the franchising process much easier than it would have been four years ago! Her new bigger warehouse, owned by her SSAS pension, in the north Midlands was identified as a hub for franchisees where they can also collect supplies for their three main offerings – craft parties, delivering floral sundries to florists in their territories and servicing commercial spaces with life-like flower arrangements and evergreens. Their liveried vans act as a mobile showroom and retail orders taken on their regular sales routes can be financed on monthly terms through the franchisor, making the business much easier to cashflow for the franchisees.

Claire has taken two franchisees through training and launch and is actively interviewing five more prospective franchisees. She can see that she'll need to recruit a team to support this growing network to ensure consistency of brand and experience for both franchisees and customers. Her craft book has been another reason for franchisees to sign up - they've benefited from regular craft party bookings in the school holidays which were a natural spin-off when parents wanted to entertain the kids but did not feel confident enough in their craft skills. Claire had learned from James that by giving away a little of her expertise, she would gain more by making her audience realise whilst they now knew enough to create some craftwork themselves, they did not have enough knowledge to teach their kids how to.

The joint venture with the floral subscription company was going well and they'd built up a healthy customer database. This, combined with the profit from her franchise and her great set of business accounts for the last few years, has helped her secure a mortgage to buy a property to call home. Claire discussed life cover with one of Frank's recommended advisors and remembering his advice, she took out a Relevant Life Assurance plan where the premiums were being paid by her company. She thought about how she had not procrastinated or drifted on the issue - something she certainly would have done before. She was feeling like a professional business owner now, in charge of her own decisions and not firefighting like she was at the beginning of this journey with Frank.

Like his sister, Mark has also kept his foot firmly on the accelerator. JS Properties now has a management team, so he's rarely needed in the business. His property mentor, Fiona, has shown him how to find, assess and offer on more complex property deals. With classroom education, onsite visits and Fiona's support, he bought a pub with a view to turning it into eight apartments. The intention was to sell those apartments to build capital and to build his knowledge too. His accountant, who specialises in property, advised him to set up a new limited company to separate it from his property portfolio which was providing him a regular monthly income - enough to be completely financially independent. Even though Frank had pointed out that all businesses were subject to the risk of disruption by external sources, he was excited to be setting new challenges for himself, but he didn't intend to be complacent.

Mark converted his and Sophie's old workplace pensions into a SSAS in the new company name - Calmer Homes Ltd. He'd chosen the name using a play on the word 'karma'. He was so thankful of the introduction to Frank from his sister. Also, since the liberal use of Claire's unique floral arrangements inside and outside of his student properties, he'd received some great feedback from his tenants - they seemed to offer a stress-relieving quality. Having something that brought another calming element to life in his properties could only be a good thing - Claire had certainly hit on something about the therapeutic nature of her products during those initial focus groups for her craft books.

The SSAS pension bought the pub outright and he used the funds to do most of the refurbishment as well. Although he'd not collaborated with Claire's SSAS when she bought her new premises, he was pleased he was building his own family trust fund. It meant that Sophie could become even more involved in his wealth journey, and he could see he would soon be involving the kids as they reached 18 years old.

As a detail-oriented person, Mark had captured all the key systems and processes on this new project, taking dozens of photographs to capture the journey. When all the apartments were sold, he was excited to find further projects. The profits were impressive - he reflected on Frank's point about how doing bigger deals was a different ball game from the smaller ones. Actually, he found there was less competition as most amateur landlords were not willing to take the risk to learn and step up to a higher level. Frank came to mind again as he recalled the early lesson about how essential it is to invest in education, coaching and mentoring. He was glad he'd followed that advice.

With his successes in student lets and his growing confidence in commercial-to-residential conversions, Mark was regularly invited to speak at property networking events, now attracting investors keen to learn his detailed approach who hoped to take a shortcut to their own property success. While it wasn't a franchise like Claire's business, he was certainly leveraging his IP. He could see a market for teaching his processes for a fee whilst attracting investors too.

Despite all of his success, one of Mark's most rewarding decisions had been something much smaller. He had spoken to some veterans at one of the FUNdraise events and they talked about the difficulties of returning to civilian life after their time in the forces. He'd decided to bring together a small panel of local veterans to help manage his portfolio. They all had so many transferable skills, becoming an immensely reliable and effective team. He wanted to do so much more and was determined the support of veterans would be a big part of his future legacy.

It's time for them to learn about investing the cashflow they've worked so hard to generate. Frank meets them in London - an appropriate place to talk investments - where he is running a seminar.

"This is a slightly larger audience than I'm used to delivering to," jokes Mark.

These are the audiences Frank has been used to for his national book launches and seminar tours for the last 10 years or so. He welcomes them backstage before the event starts. "You two will recognise some of the areas I'm going to cover in this seminar. Let's have dinner afterwards and we can catch up. The lessons come thick and fast when I'm public speaking so be ready to take notes Claire! And bear in mind, this is an audience of business owners," says Frank.

They settle into the auditorium with notebooks at the ready and they aren't surprised to see plenty of others doing the same. It strikes them that they've had five years of one-to-one coaching from a world-class wealth coach thanks to their Dad's friendship with Frank.

"I'd say it's been invaluable," says Claire, "But actually, we can put a value on it thanks to Frank teaching us how to master our finances. Here we go then!"

Frank walks out on stage to the applause of an eager crowd. His lessons are highlighted on screens in the auditorium as he talks.

> Cashflow, physical assets and paper assets:
> When I have completed or started making significant cashflow, it's time to learn how to start investing my cashflow into firstly more cashflow, secondly physical assets, and thirdly paper assets. And then do it!

"You need to steer your excess cashflow into avenues that are likely to generate more cashflow first, because as you will by now appreciate - cashflow is king. Once you've developed your cashflow through reinvesting your surplus cashflow, then it's time to think about physical assets like property. And once you have this in place, paper assets come next."

> *Business – property – stocks:*
> There are only 3 real investments that meet the rule of having both capital growth and cashflow:
>
> 1st: *Business* - low liquidity (hard to sell) and high ability to add value.
> 2nd: *Property* - medium liquidity and medium ability to add value.
> 3rd: *Stocks* - high liquidity and low, or no ability to add value.

"Business is your cash engine. It's the thing that generates the cash you'll need to invest in property and stocks. It also happens to have the highest ability to add value. That means you can generate more cashflow simply by building the business. But it has low liquidity, which means it's difficult to turn the business into cash quickly should you need to. You'd do this by selling it or selling a share of it to an investor, for instance. It could take years to find a buyer, if at all.

"Selling an investment property is likely to take months, and it depends on the property whether you can add value to it through renovation, extension or re-purposing the property from say commercial to residential.

"Stocks are easy to dispose of if you needed to, but you would have to be satisfied with what the market was willing to pay you for them. There is no or next to no ability for you personally to add value to them."

Buy retail:
My first investments will involve buying into a retail deal. Because of my lack of both knowledge and monetary capital, I will generally be paying close to or full retail for my deals.

"Retail investors invest their own money and tend to trade in relatively small amounts compared to institutional investors. When you begin investing, your inexperience means that you will likely start by buying at the same valuation as most members of the public pay - retail price if you like."

Retail business:
Here I will be buying a franchise or similar, so I won't have to learn everything at once. It's a great start. I get a system and support to help me along my way to making profits and increasing my business knowledge.

"Expect to pay the retail price for a reputable franchise and a percentage of your ongoing revenue, because this is how the franchise owner earns their money. This is the reward they get for all the hard work and investment they put in to developing and testing the business model and systems. The initial investment tends to be less for you and your return on investment is much quicker than building a similar business from scratch."

Retail shares:
Buying shares through my broker or an app, I pay full price, holding for a potential gain. While mutual funds pool money from the investing public and use it to buy investments such as stocks and bonds; a fund manager makes money by charging a small percentage management fee, a sales commission charge at the outset and at cash in. In most cases, both in the long term are better than doing nothing, but I still pay for my learning or lack of knowledge.

"You'll probably start off in the share market by buying shares at retail prices through a broker or an app."

Buying at 'wholesale' prices: In time, I accumulate enough money and knowledge where I can be offered high-risk deals and I can also start doing my own 'wholesale (lower)' investment price deals where I skip giving the salesperson or broker a sales commission.

"If you earn at least £100,000 a year or have net assets excluding property and pensions of at least £250,000, you can self-certify yourself as a high-net-worth individual (wealthier) or when you have made more than one jnvestment in an unlisted company in the last two years, you can self-certify as a 'sophisticated (experienced) investor'. Firms are allowed to advertise high-risk investments directly to high net worth and sophisticated investors. Your increased knowledge and wealth can be used to your advantage in all three of the real investments – business, property, and stocks."

> **Wholesale business:**
> Here I follow the formula of buy, build and sell. I buy well below market using little or very little of my own money, I then build value into the business with the help of a world-class business coach and make a multiple of annual profits when I sell the business.

"There are approximately three million active businesses in the UK, so you won't need to look far to find business owners who wants to retire or go back to working for someone else, because they're finding running their business too hard and stressful. It can often be cheaper than bank finance to negotiate 'vendor finance', where you pay the business owner a percentage of sales until they've received the asking price for their business.

"Key drivers of how much you'll be able to sell your business for include how well it works without you and its annual profits. As you know, your business coach will work with you on 4 Ways strategies to make the business less dependent on you and 5 Ways strategies to increase the profits. The temptation can be to sell the business too quickly, but I like to build the business for at least five years to get it working like a well-oiled machine and allow the profit-growth strategies to compound. Remember Bill Gates' wise words on how people over-estimate what they can achieve in 12 months? Let's say we achieve a 10% increase in each of the 5 Ways each year we build the business… well, that would add up to an impressive 61% increase in profits, but if I hold the business for five years, then I achieve an incredible 981% increase in profits. Couple that with improvements in people and systems and I'm likely to make more than ten times what I paid for the business when I sell it."

> **Wholesale property:**
> Now I am buying much better, I know what I'm doing and I'm making good money up front on my deals. I'm generally following the buy, renovate, remortgage formula to make my money and build my asset base.

"Your job as an investor is to buy only on logic and to avoid the emotion – look to buy below market value and in markets where you have already acquired significant knowledge. A lot of the profit is in the buying price, not the selling price, as the buyer is always the one in control. To get the best deals, you need to be willing to put in the legwork and walk away from rejected offers... as an indication of the work involved, you may find you need to view 150 properties online, visit 30 of them and put low offers in on 10 of those properties to buy one good investment property at below market value. To buy wholesale, you need to foster relationships with commercial property agents and estate agents who will then come to you first, knowing you are a serious buyer with money available.

"I like buy-to-let properties in areas where I know the tenant market well. When I've increased the value of the property through renovation and proving the income stream from tenants and that value has increased over time through increases in property prices in the market, I won't sell the property and pay taxes and commissions. Instead, I'll remortgage my property and draw down cash in a tax-free way to buy more property.

"Again, taking a long-term view and compounding are your friends here. If you buy a £250,000 buy-to-let property through a 75% mortgage (£187,500), you'll need to raise a £62,500 deposit. For that property to double in value over 10 years, you'd need 7.2% average annual property price increases. Let's assume that happens, so in 10 years' time, your property is worth £500,000 and you can increase your mortgage to £375,000 with a 75% remortgage, you'd receive a lump sum of £187,500 tax-free. And if your property doubles in value in the following 10 years, in 20 years' time you would be able to draw down

£375,000 tax-free through remortgaging and so on. So, if your business investment enables you to buy one property like that every year for 10 years, then you could achieve financial freedom in 10 years' time. I appreciate, that's calculator-land, but even with half that capital growth in property value and several months without a tenant every 10 years, you're likely to end up pleased you made the investments!"

> *Wholesale shares:*
> I am now ranked a sophisticated or professional investor and can get into deals that I never could before. I am also far more knowledgeable about financial derivatives and other deals.

"There are many instances when sophisticated investors get the jump on the general market. Take for instance where companies want to raise more cash through a stock offer. They instruct their underwriters or brokers to offer shares first to sophisticated investors or existing shareholders. And one of the advantages of buying this way is you may not have to pay brokerage fees. Secondly, the shares are usually discounted, so if you were to sell them as soon as they were listed for sale to the public, you'd make an immediate profit.

"It may be a case of the rich getting richer, but it's how the economy is structured. It needs entrepreneurs and investors and, therefore, tends to favour them.

"Derivatives are a financial product that gets its value from the value of another product, hence its name – it derives value from another product. They include mechanisms like options, warrants, and futures. They are used by investors to increase the returns and risk from their investment or to protect the value of their investment.

"Options on London Stock Exchange listed shares are often referred to as 'Traded Options', but there is no difference between a Traded Option and an Option. All Option contracts work the same way. When you understand what a stock option is, you'll also understand how an option on a commodity, like gold, works. Options come in two primary forms, 'Calls' and 'Puts'.

"A Call option gives the buyer of the Call, the right, but not the obligation, to buy a fixed number of shares at a fixed price within a fixed period of time. The seller (or 'writer') of the Call is obliged to sell the commodity or financial instrument to the buyer if the buyer so decides. The buyer pays a fee (called a 'premium') for this right. The term 'Call' comes from the fact that the owner has the right to "Call the stock away" from the seller.

For example, Vodafone June £121.04 Call option. The buyer of this Call option pays £3,700 (£3.70 per share) for the right, but not the obligation, to buy 1,000 Vodafone shares at £121.04 on or before the expiry of the option on the 3rd Friday of June for £121,040. So the maximum loss is £3,700 (the cost of the premium) and potential gains are uncapped if the Vodafone share price does well in that time frame.

"A Put option gives the buyer of the Put, the right, but not the obligation, to sell a fixed number of shares at a fixed price within a fixed period of time. The most obvious use of a Put option is as a type of insurance. In this protective Put strategy, the investor buys enough Puts to cover their holdings of their shares, so if the price of their shares falls sharply, they can still realise the agreed price per share in the Puts, thereby limiting their losses to the cost of the Put premium. Another use is when the investor speculates that the share price is going to fall significantly and through buying Puts without buying the associated shares. If the price of the share does fall below the Put price within the period of time, the investor can make the difference between the current price of the share and the Put option price through buying 1,000 shares at the current price and exercising their right to sell the shares at the agreed fixed price or by simply selling their Put option.

For example, Rolls-Royce May £110.05 Put option. The buyer of this Put option pays £3,610 (£3.61 per share) for the right, but not the obligation, to sell 1,000 Rolls-Royce shares at £110.05 on or before the 3rd Friday in May for £110,050. So if the investor has bought the Put option to protect the value of their investment, their maximum loss within the period of time is £3,610 (the cost of the premium)."

The seminar was a hit and after signing a few of his latest books, Frank joins Mark and Claire at a nearby restaurant. Mark is keen to start off the discussion:

"Tonight has got me thinking. I've been enjoying some of my new-found cashflow with the family, but I think I've been a bit wasteful when you consider what I could have been investing in instead. It's easy to get carried away with the here and now - especially when you have the kids to spoil."

Frank suggests a simple way of giving purchases a second thought.

"Before you click the 'Buy Now' button online or agree to a purchase on a whim because the kids try to guilt-trip you, click your fingers. It will make you stop and consider the purchase - you can balance the need with the want. It doesn't make you boring or mean, it just makes you think before you buy.

"However, one of the benefits of knowing the cashflow from your business or property is recurring is you can enjoy it. You can spend money on things important to you, free in the knowledge the cash will be there again the next month and the month after that. So, remember to enjoy it!

"On the flip side, it's always important to bear in mind our wealth is at risk if our roof isn't in place. Remember to keep your legal documents in good order in both your business and personal life. Keep your feet firmly on the ground and regularly review your will, powers of attorney, trusts like your SSAS pensions and so on. Remember how difficult it was when John passed away? Although he didn't have much to pass on, it was still painfully complex to organise for your Mum because his affairs weren't in order. You two have much more to make watertight after all your hard work, and taking stock of your paperwork is essential."

Legal:
The documentation that makes managing my estate easier is in place - wills, trusts, lasting power of attorney.

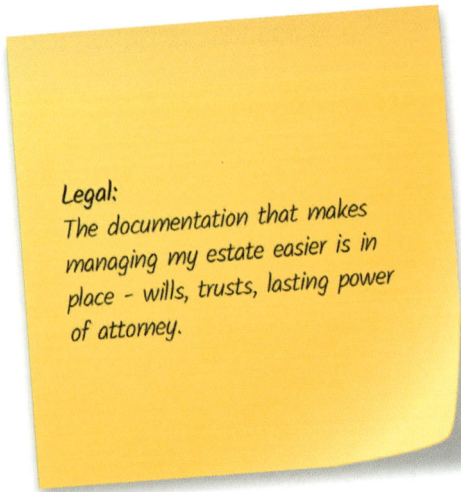

Claire and Mark are getting noticed in their community - they are not splashing the cash, but they are moving in different circles with people who also make smart financial moves. Claire talks about how an established franchise had a big noise around their flotation on AIM. She roughly knows what it's about, but can Frank enlighten her?

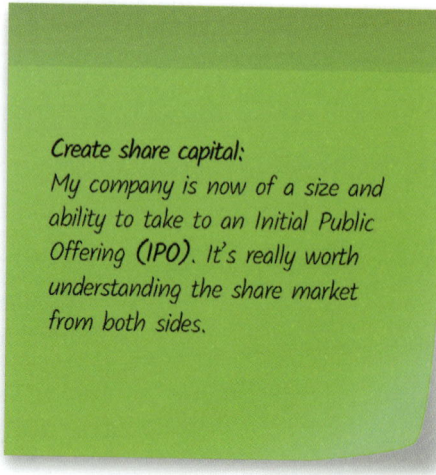

Create share capital:
My company is now of a size and ability to take to an Initial Public Offering (IPO). It's really worth understanding the share market from both sides.

"Floating, or going public, means giving a percentage of the company for purchase by the public in the form of shares. It's the process by which a privately-owned business starts to become publicly owned and is called an initial public offering (IPO). The Alternative Investment Market (AIM) is a sub-market of the London Stock Exchange (LSE) designed to help companies access cash from the public through an IPO. AIM allows these companies to raise cash by listing on a public exchange with a greater regulatory flexibility compared to the main LSE market, but an IPO does bring with it additional compliance and reporting obligations. A listing on AIM places a value on the business and there are tax incentives available for investments in AIM companies, attractive to both individual and institutional investors. The listing enhances the company's public profile and gives shareholders the opportunity to realise all or part of the value of their shareholdings. However, it would cost you several hundred thousand pounds to list your company on AIM and about £100,000 a year to stay a member.

"The attraction of buying shares in companies, like the franchise in the news for its IPO, is that the shares are usually under-priced when launched and they usually rise quickly in price when traded on the open market, making those who got in on the ground floor potential fortunes.

"Of course, you can privately sell shares in your company to individuals, but either way as the CEO of a company with shareholders, you would find yourself reporting to a board of directors and the shareholders. You'll also find your role will change with the focus shifting to prop up the share price, so it may not suit you as a business owner. However, it could bring in a lot of money for you and the company when your business is ready for a flotation."

Claire considers if her company would be suitable to raise share capital or if taking it international may be her next move. She doesn't feel the time is right to sell shares in her company and decides to do some more research into the options of master franchisees to develop other countries or putting her own employees into those countries to develop and maintain control of her franchise globally.

> **Legacy:**
> How my wealth is passed on to people and causes I care about.

"Right at the start of this journey, you wrote about your big reasons to take control and create wealth. Creating a legacy is part of that and if you're really thinking big…"

> **Legend:**
> What is the enduring contribution I want to make to society?

Mark and Claire have come a long way, but they aren't surprised they still have more to learn and more work to do. Claire observes, "I think the entrepreneur profiling tool was important to do so early on. We've both found the work we've done to get here so enjoyable because we're in our natural flow. And I think that's also helped us to do more than just build wealth, it's been good work, working for good."

Chapter 15

Reinvestment

It's seven years since John passed away and Claire and Mark meet up with Frank to toast their Dad and their own achievements since committing to a path of financial independence.

Mark's kids are now 17 and 19. One is applying to university to study property development, showing a keen interest in the family property business. The eldest is in his second year at university studying law whilst living rent free, thanks to Mark expanding his property business to several university locations across the Midlands.

"My portfolio has expanded to eight student lets but I spend more time now working as a developer with the size of projects increasing each time. My latest conversion project is an old office block near a retail centre, large enough to get permission for 24 apartments. My specifications process continues to keep our project costs down, on time and on budget. You know, whilst the growth of online shopping is a challenge for bricks-and-mortar retailers, it's bringing more properties to the market for our projects.

"My mastermind property programme is proving popular. I'm actually considering buying a commercial property, using our SSAS, to build a training suite instead of paying local hotels to run my seminars and coaching sessions. I mean, how much more has this tax-free SSAS grown compared to if I'd left it in funds at the mercy of professional fees and stock market fluctuations. Although, whilst the SSAS has facilitated a number of my projects, funding is not much of an issue now, as private investors are investing with me. I've never been a big fan of the stock market, shying away from investing in much in the way of paper assets. But I've been maxing out both my and Sophie's tax-free ISA allowance to invest in shares and diversify our investment portfolio.

"I can see I've chosen the right path and combination of assets for me - they really reflect my analytical and detail-oriented entrepreneur profile. I've got a spreadsheet for everything!"

Claire can effectively run her business from home, "My team don't really need me, but I do love leading the business now and I especially enjoy speaking at the regular franchise discovery days we arrange for prospective franchisees. My initial joint venture agreement has been formalised legally, generating a healthy recurring income from clients' subscriptions. We're adding new lines of artificial flowers and plants to the collection, using Mark's properties to showcase them to other landlords. Even though this market has grown organically, thanks to Mark, it's time to review it to see if it merits putting some serious marketing investment behind it.

"Like Mark, I've invested in the stock market, but I've built up a solid cash fund in an offset mortgage. I think it's time to reduce my mortgage to compensate for how late I got on the property ladder. Mark found me a student-let property at the beginning of the year which I own but Mark's team manage it for me. It suits me having this passive investment alongside my other interests. My SSAS has created some fantastic opportunities since it bought my new warehouse and I have a good grasp on what I can borrow money for from the pension if I need to expand, but my cashflow and profits are going well enough, so I've no immediate plans there.

"Do you remember our last meeting after your seminar? We talked about the pros and cons of taking my business to the next level. It was obviously a little early to consider listing us on AIM but there were other opportunities to think about."

"Yes, I remember," says Frank. "Most private businesses are never sold. The owners get too wrapped up in the business itself and are almost never ready for the sale. It can take several years to prepare the business with the right figures, systems and processes in place. You're both already well ahead of most here. Plus, Claire, you have a solid and growing recurring income from your subscriptions and it's clear now the business doesn't depend on you showing up every day. Most business owners are not this ready and end up selling or winding up their business because a change in circumstances forces their hand or because they're just weary of the daily grind. Even if they manage to sell their business, that set of circumstances usually results in realising a disappointing multiple of sales or profit. Frustrated by what they hoped to get for their business and what they can get, many business owners go back into their business until another external event occurs. It's a tragedy really, given the sheer hard work and risk business owners take compared to the path of being an employee.

"I'd suggest you really think hard about why you would want to sell or take money out of your business at the moment Claire. If you really want to do so, I can help you with the next steps but, in the meantime, think about the other ways owners exit their businesses.

"Some have genuine family businesses where their kids take over and run it. Obviously, you don't have children right now but, in many cases, not all kids are interested in their parent's business or don't have any entrepreneurial aspirations of their own anyway. The other option is to sell all or part of the business to employees. This can work if they have a keen interest in taking over and can access the finance to do so. It comes with challenges of course, but it can be a very successful alternative. Perhaps you can take some time to assess how you feel about your team - whether they have the desire and ability to lead and operate the business if you weren't there?

"Often, the way to maximise the value of an exit is when your business becomes a threat to another company or you have more than one potential acquirer. It's usually, but not always, a bigger business who sees something in what you've created, accelerating their growth plans. You see, people considering an acquisition aren't so much interested in the past performance of your business, but are more focused on the future. You would need to show the added value of your business being part of theirs. In fact, getting them excited about the future after a merger or acquisition is probably the only way to get a premium price for your business. It can help to engage the professional service of a business broker who is skilled in the art of selling businesses rather than handling it yourself. Apart from needing to know the finer details involved in selling a business, it's an emotional process. People see their business like a child they have nurtured from birth, and who wants to sell their baby? Finally, of course, with the recurring income and limited time you need to be working in the business, you could just keep on owning it and taking the rewards from it."

As they've just been talking about children, Claire thinks now is the perfect time to break her exciting news to Mark and Frank.

"I wanted to tell you first, I've started the process to become a parent. You know I originally thought my only option was to become a foster carer but I've found out I can apply to adopt. Back when we started this journey, I had no concept of how much control I'd have over the business. I never thought I'd be free to raise a child without being constantly drawn back into hours and hours of work. Dad seemed to be owned by his business instead of him owning it. These new-found freedoms of time and wealth mean so much to me. This evening is the perfect example of how we're able to get together as a family more - and we have you to thank for this Frank. You're a more than welcome guest for our family dinner later."

Mark adds, "That's fantastic news, sis. I love the fact I've been able to be there for my two - school, clubs, university open days. It's been really important for both me and Soph, so I totally get what you're saying."

They discussed their Dad a bit more and shed a fond tear or two. Their thoughts turn to Mum. It's her birthday later this week which is why they are all getting together for dinner later. It's partly why they've invited Frank to meet up before the others arrive.

"Mum's just about coping with Dad's pension. She'd never complain, but we'd like to get your advice, Frank, about her situation. Can we chat over a glass of wine and see what we can come up with?"

"Not a problem," says Frank. "I'm assuming you want to come up with something so Jenny doesn't feel like she's getting hand-outs or is a burden in any way? Something discreet?"

Between them, they come up with a plan to ask Jenny if they can set up a buffer account for her to tap into if she ever needs to. They decide to put a lump sum in to start it off, topping it up very month to keep her feeling safe. Claire decides to pitch it to her Mum as this being like the pension she never had.

"This isn't one of our formal coaching sessions but it's a great opportunity for me reflect on our journey together. You've both created wealth and are financially independent now. Take some time to reflect on how far you have come, but this is not the end of the road for you. You're moving to new territory now with a responsibility to give back and to pass on the wisdom I shared with you to others."

> *Responsibility comes with wealth:*
> As I'm now wealthy, I have a responsibility to teach others how to do the same with those who are ready and willing to learn and apply the knowledge – be aware most aren't and some would take you trying to help the wrong way.

"As the saying goes, 'You can lead a human to knowledge, but you can't make him think!' So choose to share your wisdom with people who realise they need help," adds Frank.

Both Mark and Claire reflect on their big goals – they've got even bigger as their freedom of time had allowed them the space to think and grow.

Claire explains, "My legacy goal has expanded to educating the huge network of parents using the craft packs and my franchisees delivering the craft parties. I'd love others to find this freedom to spend more time with their families. I've shared the foundation elements of our wealth building process in a blog, advising readers to reduce debt, do their own DEBITS, start building savings and make a will. I don't know how far I can take this, but I'm happy to have a few hundred followers - it seems like a good start. I've also found my fit at FUNdraise. We've been delivering our therapeutic flower arrangements and craft packs to some of the hospices we donate to and I want to start identifying others to donate to."

Back when Frank had asked Mark to come to one of his FUNdraise events, he hadn't got the spare time. For the last two years, Mark's been working with the FUNdraise team at every event in the Midlands. He never thought that starting his own business would actually give him more free time, not less. He's been able to achieve part of his big goal that had seemed like a dream seven years ago - remembering his grandfather through fundraising for veterans. Now he wants to take his big goal one step further and take a place on the board of trustees at FUNdraise. Frank doesn't have any plans to step down his charity efforts but hopes that Mark will take over as the head of the charity one day.

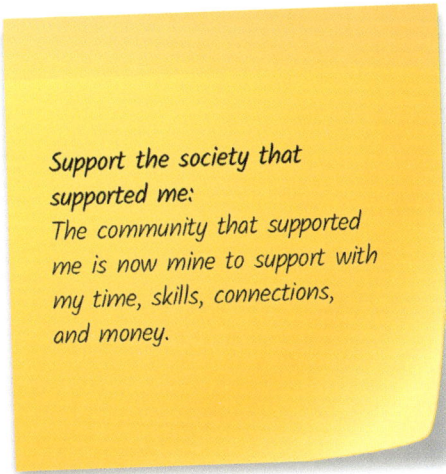

> Support the society that
> supported me:
> The community that supported
> me is now mine to support with
> my time, skills, connections,
> and money.

Claire and Mark have a gift for Frank. They know he doesn't need anything, but they wanted something to mark the occasion and decided on a set of monogram cufflinks.

"They're perfect, thank you," says Frank. "You may have learned everything you need from me but there's always more you can do. Think about those key steps you've taken and lessons you've learned over the last seven years and how you can pass them on to more people."

Claire listed the key milestones in the back of her latest notebook.

- Having a strong reason why
- Meeting a mentor and being open to receive the lessons
- Understanding my entrepreneur profile to focus on my best path
- Reviewing DEBTS
- Setting up a legally watertight roof and reviewing it regularly
- Taking stock of my pensions
- Setting up a Director's Pension / SSAS
- Investing in education
- Making many connections
- Understanding leverage and using it wisely
- Investing in property for rental income
- Building a recurring income business
- Systemising the business to free time
- Creating joint venture opportunities
- Diversifying investments to create security
- Keeping up momentum
- Learning and applying increasingly profitable strategies
- Committing to leaving a great legacy

Frank says, "I'm so proud of you. You've spent these years doing what most people will never do, to create a lifestyle most people will never have. I told you wealth building was a process and you've seen there aren't really that many lessons to learn, people to connect with or actions to take. You've encapsulated a lesson I often share with people when they ask me how to become wealthy…

Where you'll be in 5 years will depend on <u>the books you read</u>, the <u>people you associate with</u>, AND the <u>action you take.</u>

"You're living proof of this lesson. You've come a long way in seven years. It's been a pleasure to be part of your journey. Go and help more people to do the same."

Time to take action

If you're ready to commit to creating wealth, we recommend studying and applying these books - one a month for the first year of your wealth-building journey:

1. Think and Grow Rich, Napoleon Hill

2. 7 Strategies for Wealth & Happiness, Jim Rohn

3. Billionaire in Training, Bradley J. Sugars

4. Instant Cashflow, Bradley J. Sugars

5. Instant Team Building, Bradley J. Sugars

6. The Jelly Effect, Andy Bounds

7. Spin Selling, Neil Rackham

8. 5 Star Service, Michael Heppell

9. The 7 Pillars of Wealth, Kevin Whelan

10. The Automatic Customer, John Warrillow

11. Building a StoryBrand, Donald Miller

12. Instant Real Estate, Bradley J. Sugars

And remember, if you're serious about achieving your wealth, business and property goals, by far your best chance of achieving success in each field is to do what Claire and Mark did and hire a world-class wealth coach, business coach and property coach; when you do that, they can tailor their teaching to fit you. Don't be like the millions of people who pay for gym membership with great intentions, decide against hiring a personal trainer and don't get fit...

To your success,

Brad, Kevin & Ian